Duck Country

A celebration of America's favorite waterfowl

Duck Country

A celebration of America's favorite waterfowl

Michael Furtman

Ducks Unlimited, Inc.
One Waterfowl Way • Memphis, TN 38120

Willow Creek Press
P.O. Box 147 • Minocqua, WI 54548

This book is dedicated to David Zentner, a man with unsurpassed passion for both conservation and waterfowl, and whom I'm proud to call both friend and mentor.

Book Design: Monte Clair Finch

Published by Ducks Unlimited, Inc.
L. J. Mayeux, President
Julius Wall, Chairman of the Board
D. A. (Don) Young, Executive Vice President

ISBN: 1-57223-502-0
Published June 2001

Ducks Unlimited, Inc.
The mission of Ducks Unlimited is to fulfill the annual life cycle needs of North American waterfowl by protecting, enhancing, restoring, and managing important wetlands and associated uplands. Since its founding in 1937, DU has raised more than $1.3 billion, which has contributed to the conservation of over 9.4 million acres of prime wildlife habitat in all fifty states, each of the Canadian provinces, and in key areas of Mexico. In the U.S. alone, DU has helped to conserve over 2 million acres of waterfowl habitat. Some 900 species of wildlife live and flourish on DU projects, including many threatened and endangered species.

Call to Action
The success of Ducks Unlimited hinges upon each member's personal involvement in the conservation of North America's wetlands and waterfowl. You can help Ducks Unlimited meet its conservation goals by volunteering your time, energy, and resources; by participating in our conservation programs; and by encouraging others to do the same. To learn more about how you can make a difference for the ducks, call 1-800-45-DUCKS.

Library of Congress Cataloging-in-Publication Data

Furtman, Michael.
  Duck country: a celebration of America's favorite waterfowl / Michael
Furtman.
    p.cm.
  ISBN 1-57223-502-0 (hardcover : alk. paper)
1 Ducks--North America. I Title.
  QL696.A52 F86 2001
  589.4'1097--dc21
                              2001002335

Printed in Canada

Acknowledgements

If this were a scholarly text, each duck study I've mentioned would have been cited, each paper I read as research would have been acknowledged, and all the biologists who produced them would have been named. Since it is not that kind of book, I'd like to at least tip my hat to the generations of waterfowl biologists whose dedication has contributed to our impressive knowledge of ducks, and whose work laid the foundation for sound waterfowl conservation.

I've read your papers, I've enjoyed your company at conferences or in the field, and I'd just like to thank you here, on behalf of all waterfowlers (if I may be so bold), for your passion to learn about, and serve, our duck heritage. Thanks to you the world is a better place.

Ducks Unlimited, Inc.

The mission of Ducks Unlimited is to fulfill the annual life cycle needs of North American waterfowl by protecting, enhancing, restoring, and managing important wetlands and associated uplands. Since its founding in 1937, DU has raised more than $1.3 billion, which has contributed to the conservation of over 9.4 million acres of prime wildlife habitat in all fifty states, each of the Canadian provinces, and in key areas of Mexico. In the U.S. alone, DU has helped to conserve over 2 million acres of waterfowl habitat. Some 900 species of wildlife live and flourish on DU projects, including many threatened and endangered species.

Call to Action

The success of Ducks Unlimited hinges upon each member's personal involvement in the conservation of North America's wetlands and waterfowl. You can help Ducks Unlimited meet its conservation goals by volunteering your time, energy, and resources; by participating in our conservation programs; and by encouraging others to do the same. To learn more about how you can make a difference for the ducks, call 1-800-45-DUCKS.

©RICHARD DAY/DAYBREAK IMAGERY

Table of Contents

Foreword

Waterfowl are fascinating animals that are most intriguing to watch in their natural environments. They are brightly colored, easily observed, and perform a profusion of interesting behaviors. Duck admirers who look closely will see that there is a lot going on in a duck marsh. But are those towering flights in the spring courtship or territorial defense flights? Why are most male ducks so brightly colored? Why are there more males than females? What events must come together to result in those little families of ducklings that show up in the summer? Why do some species stop in certain areas to breed while others just stop to rest? Why do some nest on the ground, others over water, and still others in tree cavities? Where do they go when they leave in the fall? Ducks lovers lose sleep wondering about these things.

Michael Furtman is a duck lover who has attempted to answer these questions, which have also intrigued naturalists and professional biologists for decades. Since at least the 1930s, waterfowl have been the objects of study by wildlife managers charged with the responsibilities of assuring their abundance through habitat conservation programs and careful control of harvest. For a much longer period, waterfowl have also been intensively studied almost everywhere in the world by ornithologists interested in topics as diverse as animal behavior, nutrition, physiology, food habits, reproduction, migration, and more. As a result, there is a rich record of scientific enquiry that goes back to the nineteenth century, accumulating more information than has been amassed for any other group of birds, save domestic fowl.

Furtman is a talented natural history writer, and in *Duck Country* he cuts through much of the amassed scientific doctrine and academic jargon of scholastics to give us an easy-to-read overview of the natural history of North America's ducks. He has done considerable research in collecting the multitude of facts, observations, and interpretations offered in this beautifully illustrated book. He surely has a large reference collection of waterfowl literature, and I can personally attest to the fact that he is a persistent inquisitor of professional biologists.

Ducks are also probably the most photographed of all birds, an asset that has been beautifully exploited by Furtman and the designers and editors of this book. There is an abundance of absorbing information and exceptional images here that will stimulate readers who share Furtman's curious fascination with ducks, and I am delighted to commend this book, which is surely Mike's best yet.

Bruce Batt, Ph.D.
Chief Biologist, Ducks Unlimited, Inc.

Introduction

From the north in fall they come, careening on cold winds, sifting down the flyways from the places of their birth. They are harbingers of coming winter. They are the voice of the marsh. They are the soul of autumn. Ducks.

It has been this way for eons. Long before we drove to marshes in comfortable vehicles, long before the landscape was carved and altered, long before the attentions of private conservation organizations and governments were turned toward waterfowl conservation, ducks have made their grand journeys from north to south and back again, relying on instinct and the molecular messages encrypted in their genes. What they have seen as they have passed!

Their race has watched over the comings and goings of glaciers, flown over the last of the mastodons. For centuries, they arched above vast herds of bison, settled on bays where great whales calved. They were here when the first humans inched their way across Beringia, the land bridge that once connected North America to Asia. Ducks watched as the first sailing ships reached the shores of this continent, saw the cities develop along the coasts, were targets of hardy gunners who fed them to people in those cities. And as the ancient traditions of ducks continued, they watched over a rapidly changing world.

From a multitude of places, speaking dozens of languages, people inched across the continent on foot, on horseback, in wagons, and on rafts. For a time, not much changed for the ducks that passed overhead, but eventually these settlers changed the world that ducks had known. Silent, dark, seemingly endless forests where the wood duck and black duck nest grew loud with the ringing of axes. Estuaries where for eons canvasback and redheads had fed grew busy with the trading of ships and commercial fishing, felt the ills of factory waste. Prairies, once waist deep with

MALLARD HEN WITH BROOD: ©SCOTT NIELSEN, DU

grass, where bison, antelope, elk, and native hunters flourished, yard by yard gave way to the plow and cow.

And if they watched this all happen, so, too, some of us were watching them. Though there are those of us for whom ducks mean little, they are yet a symbol of wilderness for many of us. Just as ducks follow an ancient cycle, the people who admire them do as well.

When was it that the first human stood in awe as a roar of ducks sheeted off a quiet marsh? European cave paintings some 20,000 years old depict waterfowl—perhaps some early hunter's magic portrayed in pigment on stone. If not awe of these birds, then what would inspire a person to stand deep in a dark, dank cave, in the smoky light of an animal fat candle,

to paint such a scene? Clearly, we felt a connection with wildfowl even then, a sense perhaps of both the magic these birds entail and the gift of food that they are.

We do not know when ancient humans first hunted ducks in North America, but surely they must have for as long as they've been here, which is at least 10,000 years. We do know, however, that in what is now Nevada, native people who hunted ducks 1,800 years ago had stashed their intricate woven bulrush decoys in a pit where archeologists eventually found them. Like today's hunter who reluctantly stores his decoys for a season yet to come, these beautiful rush decoys were hidden and wrapped against the time the people would need them again.

We have watched ducks pass over us for as long as we were conscious of such things. Their passings have told us of seasons, and when those of our ancestors who lived in the North saw the ducks depart come autumn, surely they must have felt a tinge of melancholy. They could not flee like the ducks from the rigors of the winter soon to come. And as spring returned, and with it the season's waterfowl, they must have felt joy in their hearts.

Many of us are still bound by the same seasonal rhythms as our forebears, who were bound by the same rhythms that spur the ducks. Just as we cannot slip the elemental and emotional tides of the seasons, we cannot help but be buoyed by the birds that so typify a season's passing.

Aldo Leopold once wrote: "Babes do not tremble when they are shown a golf ball, but I should not like to own the boy whose hair does not lift his hat when he sees his first deer. We are dealing, therefore, with something very deep." Just as with the sighting of a deer, the sight and sound of waterfowl trigger something that lies very deep. Miracles wrapped in compact muscle and beautiful feathers, ducks are a mystery and a delight. As they pass a continent's breadth, ducks touch the lives of millions of people.

It is to that mystery and delight that this book is dedicated. Though we understand much about ducks, still there is more to learn. What we have discovered only points to what marvelous creature they are—adapted to a dizzying array of habitats, persistent in their attempt to propagate their race,

remarkable in their ability to navigate a continent and return to the exact same place from year to year. As marvelous as all this is, we should not forget that ducks do these things not for us, but to fulfill the needs of their own race. All of our science may tell us what it is that ducks do, and even sometimes how they do it, but the "why" of it all is quite simple and needs no scientific explanation. They do all that they do simply to prosper and reproduce.

Once, ducks thrived in the absence of people. Ducks have all the tools they need to do as they have always done. We can teach them nothing. But as we shape the world to suit ourselves, ducks need those of us who love them to ensure that the places they need to survive are preserved. They provide us with magic, as surely as they did long ago to the artist in the cave, or did for the weaver of those bulrush decoys. In return, we stand as guardians of their habitats.

Despite the expense and the time and the effort it takes to fulfill our end of the bargain, I know of no one involved in duck conservation who has ever doubted that we are not amply repaid. It takes but one marsh morning listening to the chatter of feeding scaup, it requires only the bright flash of a mallard's wing in flooded timber, you need only watch but once as a flock of pintails spirals down to a pond to know that ducks pay us with pure magic.

Here's to that magic.

Michael Furtman
Duluth, Minnesota

CHAPTER ONE

Spring To Life

Pushed by a warm south wind they flew over a living prairie, tan grasses bent low from winter's snow. Sparkling wetlands glinted amid the grass to the horizon and beyond, each now filled with the melted remains of what had blanketed the plains just weeks before.

As they passed, they wheeled above those that were not able to leave the prairie when winter's winds had howled down from the Arctic. Churning herds of bison grunted at this reprieve, feeding on the first green shoots, their red calves newly dropped and kept safe by mother's bulk. White-rumped antelope skittered over rises, wisping across the plains like the winds on which the ducks flew. Here also grazed scattered groups of elk, tawny and brown, the bulls' dark manes the only evidence of their sex, their huge antlers now lying on the grasslands, waiting to be gnawed by porcupines. As they flew, they saw in cottonwoods along the

For eons, prairie marshes have provided nesting habitat as well as resting stops for ducks during spring and fall migration.

rivers the pointed roofs of the people of the plains, the thin spires of smoke rising like prayers to the heavens, the dogs, the ponies, the people outside, all thankful that another spring had come.

They saw, too, the patient packs of wolves sitting on rises, watching the bison and elk, tired of grinding the bones of winter, eager to snatch a buffalo calf or a tired old elk. They heard the giant geese already on the sloughs, the mated pairs honking in defense of their breeding space, black heads with white cheeks pointed skyward as the ducks flew overhead.

And still onward they moved until the hen led her partner to a familiar marsh, flew in a grand circle around its perimeter, dropping lower and lower until, finally, with the wind in her face, she cupped her fine wings and dropped her leathery feet to drift to the water's surface with a hissing splash. Seconds behind her was the chosen drake that was her mate, skidding in to her left, attentive and alert. She was home.

She had returned to this slough, so much like many other sloughs, as if drawn by a magnet that could pull from a continent's width. What made this marsh among all others so special we cannot know, but it was hers nonetheless, a place where she had been born, where she had raised other broods in other years, where generations of her mothers had done the same. The drake was far from his birthplace, not knowing or caring where it was from here, for he, like the countless fathers before him, had followed his chosen mate to her birthplace from the dark warm marshes of the South where they had met. In this way, he ensured that the elsewhere-genes that had spawned him and that he carried would mingle with those in new places, enriching their race.

For a few moments they sat floating on cold waters in the warm sun, resting. They could hear the calling of other ducks, hear the peenting of shorebirds running on mudflats, hear the rattling of last year's dry cattails in the breeze. Then they swam slowly to where the water was shallower and warm, where they could find food and regain energy drained by the long migration, where they could find a dry shore on which to loaf in the warm sun. Though they first needed to rest, there was much to do yet. A nest site to find. Territory to defend. A mate to be protected. They of course could not think of these things, but every cell told them what to do, what was needed. Woven into each DNA molecule, woven into a long ancestral

memory, every instruction was complete, every tool refined. Now, nothing was more important than a single task: to pass on their genes to a new generation.

THE MATING GAME

As immune as we are to nature's ways, sheltered in comfortable homes, bustled across town in beasts of steel, our nights lit by the light of our own toil, we hardly feel the tug of the late winter sun as it changes angle, the days lengthen, and the nights grow shorter.

Ah, but ducks do, as do all other creatures. The ratio of the length of day to night—known as photoperiod—is a marvelous chronometer. It tells almost every other living thing on the planet "what time it is" in the cycle of life. Photoperiod triggers hormonal changes, and these hormones spur new behaviors and physical modifications. The hormones provoke the pedicles on the head of the elk to sprout new antlers. They remind ruffed grouse deep in the forest to start beating their invisible drum to attract mates. They tell fish to develop eggs, to begin to move to spawning grounds. Ducks, too, are told similar things.

Physical and behavioral changes are spurred on by hormonal stimulation sometime in late autumn, in winter, or into spring, depending on the species. The drake's nuptial plumage matures and becomes magnificent. Males develop testosterone, which inspires displaying and stimulates growth of testes. Deep inside hens, sexual organs grow from their

WOOD DUCKS: ©CLIFF BEITTEL

MALLARD: ©BILLMARCHEL.COM

In spring, the nuptial plumage of male ducks is especially vibrant, assisting them in their quest for mates. The drake wood duck (above) and drake mallard (left) shown here are resplendent in prime breeding colors.

Although they belong to different water-fowl tribes, dabblers and divers, such as the blue-winged teal (pair, above) and the redhead (pair, below) exhibit many similar mate selection and pairing behaviors

BLUE-WINGED TEAL PAIR: ©CLIFF BEITTEL

withered state, enlarging a hundredfold—their ovaries at any other time of the year are but excess flight baggage. And at the end of the breeding cycle, photoperiod (now triggering a decrease in hormones) will tell ducks when to cease mating efforts, because pursuing late nesting opportunities would be counterproductive. Though cold weather can delay these changes, and poor health can retard them, photoperiod and the chemical messages that result cannot be refused.

The first step in reproduction, once they're chemically pre-pared to do so, is to find a mate. Although ducks vary widely in behavior and location, we can generalize much about how they do this.

REDHEAD PAIR: ©WILLIAM K.VINJE

For instance, most ducks are monogamous—that is, they have one mate at a time—but unlike geese, swans, and whistling ducks, which forge lifelong (or at least long-term) pairs, they are monogamous only for a short time. Each year they will select a new mate. Pairing takes place months before actual breeding occurs, and in some species, courting begins as early as fall. For instance, mallards and gadwall pair up beginning in October and November, while lesser scaup and green-winged teal hold off until January, February, or even March. As rules of thumb, figure that larger duck species tend to pair earlier than small ones, and dabblers earlier than divers.

Why pair at all? Why not just migrate north, find a mate, and copulate there, since males don't share in the nesting or brooding duties?

Most biologists believe ducks pair so far in advance of nesting because it increases reproductive potential for both sexes. Hens can feed with less disturbance once paired, thanks to the defense provided by vigilant mates, thus building the energy reserves they'll need for the northward migration and for the rigors of nesting. Males benefit by early pairing because drakes almost always outnumber hens, and the earlier they can find a mate, the better their chances to reproduce. Like so many other species, ducks form social hierarchies, through which resources are allocated to those with higher rank. Since ducks that are paired have a higher social ranking, they have better access to choice foods, further increasing fitness for reproduction. More or better food means hens are better prepared to lay healthy clutches, and drakes are more fit to defend the hen and their breeding territory. Pairing seems to have other advantages, too. The reproductive organs of paired females are more fully developed than those of unpaired hens. Whether this is because sexually developed hens are simply more receptive to drakes, and thus pair first, or because pairing triggers faster gonad growth is undetermined, but either way, she is more fit to reproduce.

If pairing has all these advantages, why do drakes of most duck species abandon the hen once incubation begins? Because there is little advantage to him or the hen in his remaining with her. Due to predation, nesting is a dangerous affair (one reason why drakes outnumber hens), and by hanging around, the drake would diminish his own chance of survival. Unlike the larger geese, a drake duck can offer a hen virtually no protection from predators. He might, because of his bright plumage, actually attract predators to her. By early abandonment, he doesn't lower her or the brood's chances of survival, and he enhances his own because he can retreat to a protected place to undergo his molt, often done on larger waters where there are fewer predators than is the case in the nesting area. By leaving, he also frees up food resources he would otherwise consume, resources that are now the hen's and his brood's alone. And finally, even though ducks are largely monogamous, males aren't above mating with more than one female. If he leaves, he becomes available to hens who have lost their first clutch and are in need of a new mate.

EENIE, MEENIE, MINIE, MOE

Choosing a mate isn't a random event. Since the single most important thing a duck can do is pass on its genes, finding a suitable mate is critical, and female ducks have evolved elaborate means to weed out the pretenders from the contenders. That this is true has been confirmed in captive canvasback and wood duck studies. Penned hens that were given a drake of random choosing rarely laid eggs. But when allowed to select their mate, they nested normally. How are these choices made?

Male dominance probably plays an important role. Considerable evidence exists that older males pair up first, and that many yearling males go unmated. This suggests that older drakes are better at displaying; are probably better at finding (or competing for) food resources, so that they are in good physical condition and have more attractive nuptial plumage; and due to their larger body size, are better in physical confrontations with younger drakes. Since many courtship rituals involve elaborate group flights in which males compete for the hen they pursue, these competitions may even help hens decide which drake is the most agile aviator, an attractive trait because this same aerial skill is useful in her defense or the defense of her nesting site. No matter the order of importance of these traits, some combination of them indicates to the hen that a particular drake is a good choice, for it is probably up to the female to make the selection.

Ducks usually court in groups, a behavior called social courtship that likely evolved because males outnumber

NORTHERN SHOVELERS: ©CLIFF BEITTEL

BLUE-WINGED TEAL: ©CLIFF BEITTEL

Competition between courting males for available hens often erupts in physical combat between males of the same species.

AMERICAN WIGEON COURTSHIP FLIGHT. ©BILLMARCHEL.COM

Courtship rituals sometimes involve group flights in which many males pursue a single hen. Large courtship flights are especially prevalent among certain species, such as the American wigeon pictured above.

Males outnumber females in most duck species, so competition for an unpaired hen's attention often leads to aggression between potential suitors.

WOOD DUCKS: ©BILLMARCHEL.COM

A female duck makes her own displays, including the "incite" display, where she swims toward her selected mate but coyly flirts with another nearby drake.

WOOD DUCKS: ©BILLMARCHEL.COM

females, and so must compete for selection. To this end, drake ducks developed displays and plumage that are intended to be attractive and gain a hen's attention. During the courting season, the marshes have all the hormonal tension of a high school hallway, and are nearly as noisy as well. Unpaired hens call brashly to attract mates, and drakes strut about emitting weird guttural gruntings, wheezings, whistles, and even comforting cooing sounds, all while adopting strange postures, kicking up water, and picking fights.

The displays are quite similar among most Northern Hemisphere dabbling ducks, and at various times can be directed at the hen, directed at rival drakes, or directed simultaneously toward both. In any case, to be successful a drake must first attract a hen's attention and intimidate his rivals. In this melee of group sexual tension, each drake tries to direct his displaying efforts toward the hen, and each attempts to position himself near her. As you might imagine, with all this testosterone flowing, competition is fierce and fights commonly erupt. Drakes sometimes tear into each other with the savagery of a cockfight.

One of the first maneuvers in this group display (and also often performed when two ducks meet under more civil conditions) is the "drinking display," which looks just like it sounds—the drake dips his bill in the water and stretches his neck and head upward slightly as if quenching his thirst. Mutual drinking, by the way, often occurs in mated pairs just prior to copulation.

If the display is to get serious, the "mock preening" display will follow, during which the drake puts his bill under a wing and rubs it along the wing to make an *rrrrrrrrr* sound that may serve to attract the hen's attention or warn rivals to back off. When a group of drakes are all displaying toward one hen, they intensify the ritual by "preliminary shaking"—a display in which they retract their head, ruffle their body feathers, and rise above the water's surface. At some point, the quality of a drake's display must single him out, for once a hen starts to focus her attention on him, his efforts intensify even further. Now he pulls out all the stops and dips his bill to the water, shaking it from side to side before arching his back and rising from the water and emitting a loud, sharp whistle. This display, known as the "grunt whistle," is perhaps the most well known of dabbler drake rituals.

But this isn't the last trick in his bag if he has yet to sew up a commitment from the hen. He'll often follow the "grunt whistle" with the "head-up, tail-up" display, in which the rump and head are drawn toward each other, or the "nod-swimming" display, where he stretches low in the water and swims around the hen. If other drakes are still competing, he will do the hostile "down-up" display, lowering his bill to the water then jerking his head swiftly in an intimidating upward move, all while loosing a whistling sound.

Throughout this magnificent (if you're a male reader of this book) or ridiculous (if you're a female reader) ritual, the hen has been watching this male posturing while sitting pretty nonchalantly. But she knows how this game is played, and knows too that the sooner she picks a suitable mate, the better. Once she is convinced she's seen someone she prefers, she lets him know with her own displays, the most recognizable of which is called "inciting." While swimming toward the drake she has selected, she gives a flirting look at another male by flicking her head over her shoulder. To her new mate, this is a clear sign he has been chosen, and to the competitors, it means a choice has been made. Thanks to her incite display, the selected drake turns to thrash the rival to which she just has pointed—kind of a cruel joke on both drakes, when you think about it. Not that this always deters other suitors. Now that the selection has been made, the drake will be kept busy defending her against rivals, from the wintering grounds all the way north, and until the hen begins laying eggs. If egg development is the hen's largest contribution to mating, then the drake's energy equivalent is his role as defender.

The rituals of diving duck drakes are similarly magnificent or ridiculous, depending on your point of view. As with the dabblers, diver drakes often perform in groups, but their performance begins with the "neck-stretch" display, during which males extend their neck straight up as high as it will go for a several moments or more, while swimming back and forth. This is frequently followed by the "head throw," where the bill is pointed skyward and the head laid on the drake's back. While performing this, he emits an *ick-ick-cooo* sound. Female divers, like dabblers, perform the incite display to get the boys riled up.

Battling pintail drakes often pull breast feathers from each other in an attempt to make their rivals appear less suitable to courted hens.

Certain male diving ducks, such as this common goldeneye, direct an acrobatic "head throw" display toward prospective mates.

This female redhead is telling other interested drakes that she has already selected a mate, which she is identifying by tugging at his neck feathers.

REDHEADS: ©BILLMARCHEL.COM

One reason older males are selected more often may be that young drakes must perfect their displaying skills. Some studies indicate that yearling males simply don't have what it takes—perhaps they leave out subtle moves or sounds, thus decreasing their attractiveness to hens. This would suggest that courting skills improve with age. But what other factors might be at work in mate selection?

All those colorful feathers on drakes aren't there just for use by flytiers. Clearly, hens select males partially based on their physical conformity, and nothing is more obvious about a drake's physical condition than the state of his plumage. That females select mates based on outward signs of physical health isn't unusual in the animal kingdom. Cow elk actually choose their bull, not the other way around, and although a mature bull's large antlers certainly are a formidable weapon against rivals, that's not what they mean to the cow. No, for her they mean that he is wise, strong, and healthy enough to find and compete for the food resources necessary to build such impressive equipment. The condition of a drake's plumage may signal similar messages to hen ducks. For instance, one study showed that pintail drakes with the whitest breasts and the most colorful scapular feathers were selected most often by hens. It is interesting to note that competing pintail drakes often pluck feathers from their opponent's breast during fights, which might be an attempt to make their rival less sexually attractive. Hens, noting this, may take the cue that the drake with the whitest, most-intact breast feathers is a superior combatant, a trait that will enhance his responsibilities as a guardian.

So why, if displays and other mating clues are similar among species of ducks, do they choose mates of their own species?

Well, subtle differences do occur, such as vocalizations, which vary among species. In other words, though a drake of the wrong species may look good, if he doesn't say just the right thing, then the hen won't respond. In addition, imprinting is an important factor. Ducklings identify with birds of their own species by imprinting on their mother, and so once they reach adulthood they naturally are attracted to their own kind. Sometimes, though, ducks that have been reared by, and imprinted on, a hen of a different species (which occurs as a result of dump nesting) do attempt to breed with a mate outside of their own species when they mature. This is kept in check largely because it would take two "confused" birds—one of each sex—to complete the cycle, the meeting of which in populations that often number in the millions is unlikely. That said, ducks can and do reproduce with mates outside their species, and many strange crosses have been noted. This isn't much of a problem because the outcrosses are in turn, once matured, less suitable mates for all the reasons noted, but exceptions do occur. Similar species such as mallards and Mexican ducks, or mallards and black ducks, do cross with more regularity, perhaps because they look much alike and share similar voices and mating rituals. If this occurs frequently, it can dilute the gene pool, or even lower the population, of the less numerous species.

Once the initial pair bond has begun to form, it gradually strengthens through shared behaviors. The pair begin to synchronize their daily routine so that they feed, preen, and loaf at the same times and locations. They use subtle preflight sig-

READHEAD PAIR: ©ARTHUR MORRIS / BIRDS AS ART

A drake and hen redhead intensify their pair bond through intimate physical contact. After the hen has nested, however, the drake will desert her.

nals to alert each other so that when moving from place to place, they take off at the same time and don't get separated. They copulate, they call to one another when out of sight of each other, and they continue courting displays, signs that both members actively reaffirm their attachment. The bond needs to be strong, for before they nest, they must travel hundreds or thousands of miles together, survive numerous challenges, and yet arrive at the hen's place of birth together in suitable condition to reproduce.

THERE'S NO PLACE LIKE HOME

Although the strength of a hen duck's homing instinct varies depending on species, all female ducks are philopatric

MALLARD PAIR: ©BILLMARCHEL.COM

While bonded, a drake and hen, such as this mallard pair, share daily routines and will feed, preen, and loaf together.

COMMON GOLDENEYE: ©CATHY & GORDON ILLG

Mating behavior in both dabbling ducks and diving ducks, such as this common goldeneye pair, usually includes the male grasping the female by her head or neck feathers prior to, during, and sometimes after copulation.

Copulation usually takes place in the water, with the drake mounting the hen, which may temporarily become submerged during the process.

CANVASBACK PAIR: ©CATHY & GORDON ILLG

—the scientific term for the tendency to return to the place of birth, or last place of nesting, which often is one and the same.

This isn't quite expected. In birds in general, males are usually the ones with the strong homing instinct. Why is this particular sex role reversed in ducks? Probably because female ducks invest more in reproduction than do drakes, and indeed, have a much higher mortality rate during the breeding season, largely because nesting puts them at great risk to predation. Because of this inequality, it makes sense for these species to evolve in a way that increases the odds of success and survival for hens. By returning to a place with which she is intimately familiar, the hen's survival and success rates improve because she already knows the locations of good nest sites, food resources, brood-rearing ponds, and havens for molting. The very fact that she raised a brood in this place the year before, or was the result of a successful brood there last year, shows that this is an environment that has proved its worth. As the old saying goes—nothing breeds success like success.

Even though a drake invests considerable energy in defending his hen, his energy expenditures are still less than hers because his role ceases once she begins to incubate. All he needs to do after that is feed enough to regain his own vigor and supply energy for new feather growth during the molt. He doesn't need to know the territory in the same way the hen does, for he can defend her anywhere she is, and food resources are guaranteed simply because the hen has already chosen a place with ample food. The only thing he must do, so to speak, is show up and do his job.

Besides, the drake simply couldn't be philopatric. As we've seen, by forming pairs in winter, ducks improve their health and chances for reproductive success by achieving hierarchical access to foods and because the drake's defense of the hen allows her to feed in relative peace. But since males outnumber females, it is necessary for drakes to find mates as early as possible. Since most pairing takes place far away from the breeding grounds, either in the wintering areas or during northward migration, it is impossible for drake ducks to be philopatric. A drake simply must follow his hen.

It isn't that drakes aren't capable of homing, though. There is some evidence that unpaired drakes return to the area in which they were born, perhaps for the same reasons hens do. Knowledge of the surroundings and food resources would be an important advantage to a young drake who must survive for another year before he gets a chance to mate.

The rate at which hens home to a particular area does vary by species. Diving ducks tend to have strong homing instincts, regardless of the water conditions on their nesting grounds, whereas during drought, dabbling ducks more readily pioneer new areas. This tendency shouldn't be confused with a lack of homing instinct. Even during drought conditions, dabblers do indeed return home first, but if they find it too dry they move on in an attempt to find a more suitable place to breed. Compared to divers, dabblers use more-seasonal wetlands that are affected to a greater degree by annual precipitation. (When seasonal and temporary wetlands that dabblers traditionally use are dry, many of the permanent wetlands used by divers still have water, so divers have less need to disperse.) This flexibility is an asset, but it doesn't completely offset the reproductive advantage of nesting in familiar surroundings. Often, when ducks disperse and overfly the prairies in years of drought, nesting success in the new area is lower, and broods are smaller. But even among dabblers, the strength of the homing instinct varies. One recent study in North Dakota indicated gadwall and mallards displayed strong philopatry, while blue-winged teal did not. Perhaps this shouldn't surprise us, because the tendency of blue-winged teal to move during periods of drought to areas with good water conditions—even far outside their normal breeding range—is well known.

NEST SITES: IT'S THE QUALITY THAT COUNTS

When a hen leads her drake back to her ancestral breeding area, she does so because she knows that it can provide all that she and her brood will need: a good nest site, fertile wetlands rich in foods, other wetlands where she can raise the brood, and a safe place to molt. It makes little difference whether the

NORTH CENTRAL NORTH DAKOTA WETLAND COMPLEX: ©BILL VINJE

hen is a wood duck nesting in a river-bottom forest in Illinois, a mallard on the prairies of Saskatchewan, or an eider on the Arctic tundra. The elements needed for success are the same no matter where on the continent a duck nests, though the particulars might be somewhat different. Though ducks no longer fly north over an unbroken prairie, and their options are now often severely limited or limited in quality, they still have an ancestral picture in mind of just what kind of habitat they need. They can no more change their needs than they can change species. But what is it that they are looking for?

For years, waterfowlers have heard the term "wetland complex," and this is what the ducks have as a goal. Though its location may change—it may be a fertile river delta in the

YUKON DELTA NATIONAL WILDLIFE REFUGE: ©GARY KRAMER

Wetland complexes fulfill a variety of needs for waterfowl and are among the most productive breeding habitats in North America.

Canadian northwest, a sweeping tundra pockmarked with ponds, or the potholes of the prairie and parkland region—this complex is exactly that: complex. It isn't just a wet spot. It isn't just a nest site. It isn't just a place to brood young ones. It is all of that and more, and the quality of it greatly affects the success of the breeding season.

A wetland complex, particularly on the prairies, exists where temporary, seasonal, and semipermanent wetlands are all found near each other, and the best complexes have many temporary or seasonal ponds within a half mile or so of a bigger, more permanent pothole. If you have all these types of wetlands together, you'll have not only good duck production, but also more total ducks, since the greater the number of ponds, the more territorial pairs an area can support. In some parts of the rolling hills of the Missouri Coteau region of North and South Dakota and Saskatchewan, there are in excess of 100 potholes per square mile of land. It should be no surprise, then, that this region also supports extremely high breeding densities of ducks.

Having just one type of wetland isn't enough for most species of waterfowl. An isolated temporary pond may be used by migrating ducks, but it won't contribute much to waterfowl production unless a larger, semipermanent pond is nearby for brood-rearing purposes. And no amount of water makes much of a difference if there isn't good nesting cover nearby. To have good duck production, you need large blocks of unbroken nesting cover that are undisturbed during nesting season.

Ducks don't rationalize this, of course, and because we've destroyed so much of the wetland and grassland base in significant parts of their most important breeding range, they have to make do with what we've left them. But when all the important elements of a wetland complex are intact, ducks are capable of impressive reproductive efforts, and the success of those efforts breeds more success—the daughters return to where the mother hatched them. It may be pure homing instinct, or there may be some freedom of choice in the selection process, but in any case, a hen duck knows a good place when she sees it.

The shallow wetlands—the ones most frequently drained or plowed, though they may dry up by June—are particularly important to nesting hens. Some ducks store important nutrients during the winter that will aid them during egg production, while others (usually the smaller species) do not. Both types, however, need small, shallow, temporary wetlands on which to feed when they first return north, because these warm up the fastest, and produce the greatest amount of aquatic invertebrates on which the nesting hen feeds. Calcium is gained for eggshells, and the high-protein diet fuels the hen's egg production and restores lost vigor. Without these important wetlands, she may start the nesting cycle with a nutrient deficit. That's why it doesn't hurt if these temporary wetlands dry up early in the summer—by that time the hen will be sitting on her eggs, and the territory the pair had set up at that little wetland will have served its purpose. Once the ducklings are hatched, the hen will move them to a different, usually somewhat larger, wetland (or series of wetlands) where the ducklings can mature.

Of course, the hen also needs a place to nest, which is why the quality of the uplands or emergent vegetation nearby is so important. Nest sites vary, but can be broken down into three categories: dry upland areas (with dense cover of grass or brush), vegetation (such as bulrush) over water, or tree cavities (or artificial nest boxes). Some duck species are restricted to one type of nest site; others are more flexible and can use more than one. The ubiquitous mallard has been known to nest in uplands, over water, and in baskets on poles. But the key feature of all nest sites is that they provide a secure (relatively speaking) place for the nest and for the hen, who must sit tight despite weather and predators for nearly a month.

Upland sites can include everything from a nest under the sweeping branches of a spruce tree for a black duck in Maine to a mallard hen tucked deep in a snowberry bush in Saskatchewan. Nearly every study ever done on ground-nesting ducks shows that nest success is highest where the cover is thick enough to present some kind of barrier to the movements of predators. And while the density of the nesting cover is important, so is the amount. A narrow band of otherwise decent cover surrounding a pothole amid 100 acres of plowed field is easily searched by predators, no matter how thick it is —a condition that is far too common these days, especially in prairie Canada. But vast acres of cover, even if slightly thinner,

GADWALL DRAKE: ©CLIFF BEITTEL

Shallow wetlands are particularly important to ducks, especially nesting hens, which require supplementary calcium and protein for egg laying.

MALLARD BROOD: ©GLENN D. CHAMBERS, DU

Ducks utilize a variety of nesting sites, including uplands (mallard hen, above), over-water nests built of mats of floating vegetation (canvasback hen, right), and tree cavities (wood duck hen, far right).

provide good safety, since hens and nests can escape detection from predators through the sheer randomness of it all, which is why the millions of acres of grass planted in the Dakotas under the federal farm bill's Conservation Reserve Program has helped boost duck numbers so tremendously in recent years. Biologists also believe that large expanses of grasslands tend to have a predator community dominated by coyotes, which seldom prey on ducks or eggs, while fragmented grasslands tend to have more foxes, skunks, and raccoons, which target ducks and eggs.

Overwater nesters take advantage of dense rushes and reeds in the same manner upland nesters use dense grass or bushes. By building nests among the thick stems on a mat raised above water level, these ducks also use vegetation to provide security from predation. Since their nests are often surrounded by a moat of water, security is further enhanced.

The most important thing for both upland and overwater nesting ducks isn't the exact species of plant in which they nest, but how tall and how thick it is. They can and do make use of a wide variety of grasses, forbs, and shrubs, as long as it is sufficiently protective.

Cavity nesters have their own set of criteria. A good nest cavity shouldn't be so far from water that the overland trek by the ducklings is fatal, should be high enough above the forest floor to deter some predators, should have an entrance just large enough for a hen to squeeze through but not so large that a raccoon can gain access, and should be deep enough inside that the hairy arms of grasping predators can't reach in and snatch up a meal.

When you pause to think about it, a duck's needs aren't so very different from our own—a secure place to live and raise offspring, and the food and water resources necessary to

CANVASBACK HEN: ©GLENN D. CHAMBERS, DU

WOOD DUCK HEN: ©DU

accomplish that task. The higher the quality of these requirements, the more likely the chance for success. And it is also quite remarkable that almost every possible ecological niche is filled by one species of duck or another—small marshes, big sloughs, tundras, forests, upland sites, or tree cavities. This diversity blesses us with more kinds of ducks, and more total numbers of ducks, than we'd have if all species had the same needs.

It is also a pretty simple equation: The more we change their habitat from that evolved, ancestral "picture" of it in the duck's mind, the greater the odds for reproductive failure. While ducks are in many ways remarkably versatile, they still can't modify their nesting, brooding, and molting requirements beyond their genetic boundaries. A duck like the pintail, which once nested on pristine shortgrass prairies but today is attracted to a soon-to-be-plowed wheat stubble field because it best fits the "picture" of the long-gone prairie, nests at great risk. The plow will inevitably come, and the nest, and perhaps the hen, will be lost.

KEEP OUT! NO TRESPASSING

If you've found a place that has all the requisite criteria for reproduction, you might just want to stake it out. And in fact, ducks do just that. Most are territorial, and they attempt to keep others of their own species out. Although some species nest in colonies, the majority of species are solitary nesters, and even when these do gather in larger groups to nest, it is usually because the conditions are so favorable at that spot that they are willing to put up with each other. This situation arises when wood ducks find many good cavities, or a bunch of nest boxes, in close proximity, or when prairie ducks forgo solitary nesting to take advantage of an island in a pothole that provides them with exceptional safety from predators.

The norm, however, is each pair to its own space, and even when a species like gadwall or mallards do nest in colonies on islands, the mated pair will probably stake out a territory along some section of shoreline across from the island that they will defend as a place to mate and rest.

A breeding pair will have two pieces of turf. The first is their "home range," which is simply the area where they can be found

A drake wood duck stays alert to protect his hen from the advances of other drakes as she inspects a wood duck box for a potential nesting site.

on a day-to-day basis during the prenesting period and where all of their activity takes place. It isn't usually defended against intruders. They will also have a "territory," which is a smaller part of the home range that the drake will defend by attacking and driving away another pair, drake, or hen of his own species. Territories usually incorporate the place where the pair copulates, where they feed and rest, and where their nest site has been established. Defense of this space usually ends sometime early in incubation. The most common type of defense is a pursuit flight—sometimes called a "three-bird flight"—during which the drake, protecting his territory, chases the hen of another mated pair out of the area. The third bird in the flight is the drake paired with the hen being pursued.

REDHEAD THREE-BIRD FLIGHT: ©BILLMARCHEL.COM

Not that all duck species are as territorial as the next—the drakes of lesser scaup and canvasback, for instance, tend to defend a moving territory that is essentially his mate and a small area around her, no matter where she is, rather than a piece of ground or patch of water. Others, like the mallard, defend a specific area, but their territory and that of other pairs may overlap, and conflicts only arise when both try to occupy the same place at the same time. Some species have territories with strict borders that do not overlap with those of others of their kind, and these species defend this space aggressively. Shovelers and blue-winged teal fall into this category. As a rule, it is thought that larger species have larger territories, and that dabblers are more territorial and more aggressive in defense of their turf than divers.

Of course, there are always exceptions. Pintails, though they are large dabblers, aren't particularly aggressive in defending territories. Although a drake pintail will attack another male when spurred on by his mate's incite behavior, pintail hens actually appear to be more aggressive in defense of their mate than are the drakes. And the rule of tolerating other ducks outside your own species is sometimes bent, particularly when ecologically similar species bump into each other; where the ranges of blue-winged teal and cinnamon teal overlap, interspecies conflicts arise, as it also does where mallards and black ducks coincide.

You might wonder why drakes defend a territory in the first place. After all, resources don't seem to be in all that much of a short supply. One big reason is simply to provide the peace a hen needs from amorous suitors so that she can feed at a time when her nutritional requirements are at their peak. Another is that by keeping those suitors away while she is fertile, the drake ensures that she has his offspring, not those of someone who just sneaked in. In many species of ducks, given half a chance, roving groups of bachelor males will participate in what used to be called a "rape flight,"and is now called forced copulation. They will pursue a hen until she is exhausted, forcing her to the ground or water, where they will copulate with her in succession. Occasionally, the hen is even drowned during the process. Finally, territorial behavior helps space ducks out over the available habitat, which is one key reason why protecting whole complexes of wetlands is important. The more wetlands available, the more room there is for territories and pairs. It's pretty simple.

As a general rule, waterfowl biologists say that 10 one-acre seasonal or temporary wetlands will attract three times more pairs of breeding ducks than will one 10-acre wetland, giving each their space to set up a territory.

THE INCREDIBLE EGG

As they say, good things come in small packages. From the time of her arrival on the nesting grounds, a hen is busy preparing to lay her eggs. Days are partially spent in low flights over her territory, looking for nest sites, and she will drop down and walk around to inspect likely spots, seeking

Male waterfowl are among the few birds that actually have a penis (below), and penetration of the hen (above) is required for fertilization.

just the right place. When not doing this, she feeds heavily on aquatic invertebrates, accumulating the nutrients needed for egg production, while the drake jealously guards her. And of course, the pair copulate during this period of fertility, an act that usually takes place on the water, with the drake mounting her from behind. Male waterfowl, by the way, are among the few birds that actually have a penis, and penetration of the hen is required for fertilization. Most birds simply press their cloacal (the cloaca is a common chamber into which the intestinal, urinary, and reproductive canals discharge) regions together to mate.

The road from ovarian follicle (female gamete) to a completed egg is an interesting one. Even though hens have two ovaries, only the left one normally develops, which may be an adaptation to reduce total body mass (to make flight easier), or to ensure only one egg develops at a time. If two eggs developed simultaneously, they would lie side by side within her, taking enormous room and perhaps fracturing each other during movement.

When the pair mates, some 8 billion sperm are transferred to the hen and stored in her vaginal pouch. This sperm can remain viable for up to two weeks. During ovulation, when a follicle reaches maturity, an ovum is fertilized by some of this sperm in an area called the infundibulum. It then passes into the magnum, where it remains for about four hours and acquires the egg white, which supplies water to the embryo and acts as a cushion. The ovum then passes into the isthmus,

where it remains for about 15 minutes, acquiring the membranes to build a shell, and then moves to the uterus, where it spends some 18 to 20 hours as the shell is formed. Finally, it moves to the vagina, where it will remain until strong muscles help push it into the nest.

Compared to those of other birds, the eggs of waterfowl are large in relation to the female's body mass. Big eggs mean relatively big offspring, which are better at regulating their temperature (which increases survival). Because of their large size, these eggs also contain a lot of yolk, which gives young waterfowl a chance to survive should food not be readily available upon hatching, since some of the yolk remains as a source of nutrients in the abdomen of the young. The duckling actually grows around the yolk, which is why a portion is left inside it when it hatches. The shell, by the way, is the original "breathable-waterproof" protective outer covering. Composed of calcium carbonate crystals aligned in a matrix, the shell is porous enough to allow gases inside the egg to escape (after all, the duckling is alive in there, and while breathing, produces carbon dioxide), while providing durable protection from outside elements.

Producing such large eggs also requires great stores of the hen's energy, which is why her nutritional demands are so high during the egg-laying period. The number and quality of the eggs she will lay are dependent upon the quality of the food available to her, so even subtle changes in wetland quality that might not be visible to us, but which affect invertebrate

MALLARD NEST: ©BILLMARCHEL.COM

life, can ultimately influence the number of ducklings that will hatch. Some factors that can influence wetland fertility are whether or not it was farmed (plowed) the year before when dry, or if herbicides, pesticides, fertilizers, and sediment have drained into it from nearby farm fields. In addition, since many species begin to store these needed nutrients during the winter or while migrating, the quality of habitat in such faraway places as Louisiana or California can also affect reproductive success months later and thousands of miles away.

Once the first egg is being formed, the hen gets serious about building her nest, though she may not complete it until after several eggs have been laid. Because of the energy demands of laying eggs, she can only deposit one per day, which is usually done in the morning. Sometimes a hen will skip a day in this cycle. In any case, she'll continue laying until her clutch is complete, the size of which varies by species, but

MALLARD HEN ON NEST: ©MASLOWSKI PHOTO

A typical dabbling duck nest starts as a "scrape" where the hen clears away existing ground cover, then adds pieces of vegetation to form a nest as she lays her eggs, usually at the rate of one per day. When the clutch is almost complete, she will pluck down from her breast to act as additional insulation for the eggs.

WOOD DUCK HEN IN NESTBOX ©MASLOWSKI PHOTO

to lose more body weight during the process. When a hen does leave the nest to feed or drink, she may fly directly from it, but most often she will walk a short distance before taking wing. When returning, she also lands a distance away, and walks to the nest, probably in an attempt to confuse predators as to its actual location. About this time, the drake of the pair begins to lose interest, and the pair bond dissolves. He flies off to find hens still in need of a mate, to feed and regain his own lost vigor, and to prepare to molt.

Most nests are a simple cup, woven of material within bill's reach. But as she incubates, the hen plucks down from her breast and adds it to the nest, which she'll spread over the eggs to keep them warm when she leaves to feed. By baring her breast, she also allows for better skin contact with the eggs, which helps heat transfer. Using her bill, the hen occasionally rotates each egg, and also moves the outer ones to the center, and vice versa. This helps ensure that during the course of incubation each egg gets equal contact with her breast for warmth, so all of the eggs develop at the same rate. Moving them around also helps to keep the embryo from sticking to one side of the egg. Depending on the weather, she'll alter the "tightness of sit." She'll take advantage of warm weather by stretching or feeding more often, but will hunker down tighter, and for longer periods, on windy days, or when it rains or snows. If all goes well and she escapes the predators that are actively searching for her, she'll continue the long bouts of sitting until the eggs hatch, some 20 to 30 days later, depending on the species.

is somewhere between 6 and 12 eggs, on average. Older, more experienced hens tend to lay larger clutches than do young hens. Incubation begins gradually, with the hen spending increased time on the nest as the laying continues. Freshly laid eggs are remarkably cold tolerant, so initially she doesn't need to keep them warm. In fact, it would be counterproductive. If she began incubating as soon as the first egg were laid, it would hatch many days before the last egg. By waiting to incubate until the last egg is laid, the eggs of ducks hatch synchronously, even though they may have been laid 10 or more days apart.

During incubation, a hen will only take one or two short breaks per day to feed, and so must rely heavily upon stored body fat for her own nutritional needs. Large duck species tend to sit longer each day than small ones, and are able to do so because they are better at storing fat reserves. They also tend

Many ducklings (above), eggs, and hens are lost to predators during the nesting period. Mammalian predators such as skunks and raccoons (right) take a huge toll of duck eggs every year.

©PHOTOS-BY-RM.COM

Many nests, and a considerable number of hens, are lost during this period, and the rate of failure has been increasing for some species as habitat alterations have caused changes in the number and kind of predators on the nesting grounds. For instance, historically the raccoon was rarely found on the prairie, but human changes to prairie habitat have allowed it to expand its range, introducing a very efficient predator to prey upon species that have evolved little defense against it. Since raccoons are fond of water, even the eggs of overwater nesters aren't safe. Similarly, the population of red foxes on the prairie has flourished in the absence of the larger canids—coyotes and wolves—which if humans had not removed them, would have kept red fox numbers in check.

If a hen loses her nest early in the incubation cycle, she will often attempt to lay a second clutch. A few may even attempt

RACCOON: ©F. EUGENE HESTER

26

RED FOX WITH GREEN-WINGED TEAL: ©GARY KRAMER

BLACK RAT SNAKE IN NESTING BOX: ©JACK DERMID

Red fox kill hens as well as eat their eggs. Snakes are also egg predators and are often known to invade wood duck boxes when searching for a meal.

to lay a third. Current studies in Canada show some mallards will try four, five, or six times. But with each subsequent attempt, clutch sizes will be smaller, probably reflecting the decreasing energy reserves of the hen. At some point, she ceases to attempt to renest, either because she simply doesn't have the energy needed, or because there is insufficient time to raise a brood to flight stage before the arrival of autumn. It is this ability to renest, however, that provides so much resiliency to duck populations. In some years, poor conditions reign early in the season, and things can actually get better later on. If ducks weren't able to take advantages of these situations in the course of one breeding season, they'd have to wait a whole year before attempting to nest again. They are also a long-lived group of birds, and many experienced hens simply avoid the risks of nesting during drought so they can survive until conditions are better during subsequent years.

BROODS

The days of summer are at their greatest length. May has passed into June, and all across the breeding range, hens are sitting tight, nearing the end of the nesting cycle. About two days prior to hatching, the ducklings inside the eggs actually begin to converse with each other and the hen. Inside their liquid world, they peep faintly and scrape their bills against the inside side of the shell, an action that is known as "pipping." These furtive sounds may tell the less developed ducklings to hurry along to help synchronize hatching. Even though a nest may have a dozen eggs laid a dozen days apart, all will hatch on the same day. And if you think the first egg laid would be the first to hatch (because it is oldest), you're wrong; actually, the last egg laid hatches first because it never had a chance to cool. In response to the pipping and peeping in the eggs, the hen, who has been silent her whole time on the nest lest she attract predators, now begins to talk to them in a low voice, so that even before the ducklings have emerged they've begun to imprint on their mother.

In the full lushness of summer, millions of tiny miracles finally occur as ducklings struggle to emerge. With truly great effort, considering their small size and tight confines, the ducklings begin to chisel their way out of the egg, using a small knob on their bill known as an egg tooth. Once they have managed to create a star-shaped crack in the shell, the duckling rotates within the egg and chips away in a circle until it separates the larger end, which falls away. Emerging exhausted and wet into a bright new world, the duckling dries off, fluffs up, and takes a nap. We'd probably do the same thing.

Unlike the young of songbirds, which arrive naked and feeble, the offspring of waterfowl are "precocial"—which means they are able to maintain a constant body temperature, feed themselves, and move about. At birth, the sex ratio is usually about 50:50. Within about 24 hours of hatching, many will be led on the longest overland journey of their life, sometimes walking up to a mile from the nest site to the place the hen has chosen to brood them. Because of the need to make

Hatching is facilitated by a chisel-like egg tooth on the tip of the bill of emerging ducklings.

WOOD DUCK DUCKLING AND KINGFISHER: ©BILLMARCHEL.COM

A wood duck duckling takes its first look at the outside world as a kingfisher perches on the roof of its nest box.

Led by the hen, ducklings hatched in upland nest sites must travel overland from their nest, sometimes for distances up to a mile, before reaching brood-rearing water the hen has selected for that purpose.

BLUE-WINGED TEAL BROOD: ©BILLMARCHEL.COM

A canvasback hen and her brood loaf on a fallen log. Should a predator appear, the surrounding open water offers these diving ducks an escape route to safety.

CANVASBACK BROOD: ©GLENN D. CHAMBERS, DU

these overland treks, the legs of ducklings are very large compared to the rest of their body, and will grow more slowly so that their proportions catch up.

Muttering gentle sounds to them as they waddle through the grasslands, across the springy tundra, or through the forest, the hen leads her brood over hill and dale to a special wetland she has chosen, perhaps on low flights during her brief feeding forays. This is known as a brood wetland, and because her brood's needs will change as they grow, the hen may move them through a succession of wetlands as the days go by. During this time, most hens are fearless against all comers in defense of their broods—sometimes with great ferocity, at other times using the classic feigned "broken-wing" injury to attract the predator toward her while her ducklings scurry

into deep cover. The hen will even defend her offspring against other ducks in order to ensure that they will have the best access to foods and loafing areas. Her wisdom at this point helps increase the brood's success rate—those hens that are the most alert, are the bravest, and know where the best foods and wetlands are to be found probably have the highest brood survival rates. She has already invested great stores of energy and effort to fulfill her reproductive urge, but the journey to replacing herself won't end until at least one of her ducklings survives to flight stage.

What makes good brood habitat? First, it must provide security from predators—in the form of good emergent vegetation as hiding cover for dabblers, or open water to escape to for divers. Second, it needs to have suitable loafing areas.

Feeding almost continuously throughout the day allows ducklings to grow rapidly and reach flight stage in 50 to 60 days.

Some hens select loafing sites that are elevated and have little cover so that they can spot predators more readily. Third, good brood habitat must also have an abundant supply of food (as in lots of bugs). Ducklings are almost completely carnivorous for the first two weeks, and for some species, much

longer. They eat a wide range of insects and aquatic invertebrates, which provide the high-protein diet they need to grow rapidly, and they feed through about 60 percent of the daylight hours. Surprising as it may seem, ducklings near the Arctic Circle actually grow faster than their counterparts—even of the same species—to the south, since they can take advantage of the nightless days to feed more frequently.

At this stage, ducklings are veritable feeding machines, able to swim and dive in the capture of food, and even though they peck randomly at first to see just what is edible, it isn't long before they know to select particularly choice morsels, such as aquatic beetles and freshwater shrimp. They need to eat well, since much depends on the quality of their diet. Autumn isn't that far away, and in just a short period they need to grow to full adult size and grow full plumage. What they manage to do in about 50 or 60 days takes a puppy 12 months, and a child about 16 years. In addition to how well they grow, their very survival during this period is also related to how well they eat—the faster they grow, the lower the mortality rate because the bigger they are, the sooner they can fly, and the harder it will be for something to catch and eat them. It may seem like a lot to ask of a bunch of bugs and some watery greens, but even the ducklings' future reproductive potential is influenced by the quality and quantity of their food at this early stage. Those ducklings that eat and grow well will be larger as adults, and since larger hens produce larger clutches, and bigger drakes are better at competing for mates, the race to reproduce can be won or lost at the brood pond supper table.

As the summer progresses and the ducklings grow, they begin to switch to vegetable foods, and at the same time, the bond between mother and young weakens. Hens of some species will abandon their young as early as four or five weeks after hatching; others will stay with them until they are nearly ready to fly. But at some point, each hen must tend to her own needs. While she has been nesting and brooding, drakes and unpaired adults have been off molting, and even her own young are working through a succession of plumages on their way to growing their flight feathers. She too must complete the molt, and so sooner or later she will leave the ducklings to fend for themselves in a fairly danger-ous world. Even those hens that do not abandon their broods spend an increasing amount of time away from them as they mature. Unlike geese and swans, which retain the family unit right through the autumn migration, autumn groupings of ducks are related more by chance than by family ties.

This flocking behavior actually begins quite early in life, for it is not uncommon for two or more broods to gather into larger groups called "crèches," which may or may not be attended by a single hen. Although crèches occur more frequently among species like mergansers or eiders than dabblers, it has been noted in just about every duck species. Crèching probably serves several needs. Just as herding provides safety for some ungulates, ducklings benefit by the alertness of many eyes and ears to warn of trouble. And should a predator strike, any one individual is buffered against attack simply because the more ducklings there are in your group, the lower the odds that you'll be the one to get snatched. Crèches, because they are attended by only one or two hens (which may not even be related to the ducklings), also give the mothers of the broods more time to feed undisturbed so that they can recover lost energy.

As the summer wears on and the sun beats down, the small wetlands so popular as breeding sites have largely dried up. Hens have moved their broods from one wetland to another in an attempt to continue to find high-quality foods for their rapidly growing offspring. The ducklings have done their part by feeding incessantly, and by 20 days of age the first tufts of real feathers start to show through their faded coat of down. It'll only take about two more weeks before half their now elongating body is feathered, and by 40 days only a few small tufts of down are still visible among the feathers of their back. Amazingly, it takes just 50 days for the ducklings of most species to be fully feathered, and although flightless at this stage, the day of first flight is not far away. The young of most duck species can fly by about two months, though some teal lift off at 35 days, and straggler canvasback sometime need 68 days. In any case, the ability to fly comes none too soon. If you've been watching the calendar as we've chroni-cled these events, from nesting in May and June, through an incubation period that lasts three or more weeks, and then the 50 to 60 days to flight stage, you will have noted that it is already sometime in August. For ducks in the North Country, autumn is just around the bend. Migration for some may just be a matter of a few short weeks away.

Molt: Dressing Up for the Flight South

Of course, in order to fly the length of a continent, ducks not only need to put on stores of fat, but also must fine-tune their flying apparatus—their feathers.

If breeding is an energy-intensive endeavor, it doesn't surpass the molting process by much. Feathers are almost entirely composed of protein, and in order to grow a whole new set, ducks must have lots of high-protein foods, in the form of either—you guessed it—aquatic invertebrates or quality wet-

This drake mallard in eclipse plumage will remain flightless for about three weeks, until his molted flight feathers are replaced with new ones.

land vegetation. And unlike geese, swans, and whistling ducks that molt just once per year (also in the summer), most ducks undergo two molts. The year-round plumage of geese and swans is called "basic" plumage by biologists, and the birds simply molt from one basic plumage to another basic plumage. Ducks, however, have a more complex molt pattern that generally consists of conspicuous male coloration during the breeding season, followed by a drab, more camouflaged set of feathers in mid- to late summer, which is held for several months in some species. Although hens are drab-colored year-round, they too have two exchanges of body feathers. They acquire an even drabber coat for the nesting season during late winter or early spring, which is replaced during the summer molt after they've completed their breeding chores. Thus the principal difference between the two sexes is the timing of this molt—both undergo a molt in the summer, with drakes molting again into breeding plumage in fall and winter, and hens molting into drab camouflage later in the winter.

For both sexes, the summer molt leaves them flightless. One might ask why ducks would evolve in a way that would leave them unable to fly. Grouse, for instance, are never flightless during their molt, shedding and growing flight feathers in a sequence that allows them to always take wing, even if flight is somewhat labored.

The answer seems to be in the habitats in which ducks are found—wetlands, ponds, and lakes. A grouse has but one means of escaping a predator—by taking flight. Ducks, how-

STAGING DUCKS; ©GLENN D. CHAMBERS, DU

ever, can molt on water, where they can swim away, hide in emergent vegetation, or dive. Food is also readily available without the need to fly. The combination allows ducks to have a simultaneous wing molt. The flightless period varies by species, and even within species. Lesser scaup may be flightless from 14 to 21 days, whereas wigeon can't fly for a month. Most other species fall somewhere in between, and a good average would be about 26 days. Hens with broods begin molting while caring for them, but delay the wing molt (and flightless period) until done with their brooding chores.

Because ducks must eat a lot during this period, and because their flightlessness leaves them at risk to predation, the quality of the wetland chosen for the molt process is important. If the resources needed aren't found right near the place of breeding, ducks will undertake a molt migration (primarily males and unpaired hens—the nesting hens pretty much must molt where they breed) to a better location. Ideal molting locations for dabblers and divers have shallow water, abundant food, and good hiding cover, and are remote enough so that the birds won't be disturbed. Divers also tend to prefer larger bodies of water. Eiders, on the other hand, perform long molt migrations out to sea. Even among prairie ducks, some molt migrations can be fairly lengthy; diving ducks frequently fly north to the lakes of the southern boreal forest to perform their wing molt.

By the end of this cycle, drakes will have the drab feathers referred to as "eclipse" plumage, which will gradually be replaced during the fall with their gaudy breeding plumage. For all ducks, the molt is a process by which old, worn feathers are replaced sequentially with new ones over the entire body, and even the down is replaced. The sequence differs between males and females, but is gradual for both—it wouldn't do to be naked! With the completion of its molt, the duck is ready for the long migration south.

There is a difference between juvenile and adult molts that lends a useful clue to determining the age of ducks in hand, at least through early autumn. As ducklings grow their first real coat of feathers, the down is pushed out by the shafts of the new growth. On the tail, the down frequently remains attached to the tips of the new tail feathers (called retrices), only to later break off. This leaves a notched tip to the retrices of juveniles, while the tail feathers of adults have a round or pointed tip. (The tail feathers of young ducks are replaced with new ones lacking the notch in late autumn or early winter.)

Summer is rapidly coming to a close. The surviving ducklings are now nearly indistinguishable from adults in size and coloration, and their parents have completed their molt.

Nights are cooling, and there is a tension in the air for all species that live and breed in the North—winter is coming, with its frigid winds, food shortages, and long, dark nights.

Ducks feel this tension too, although their reaction to it is different from those of many of the species that surround them. They are able to escape, are able to fly to where it is soft and warm, where the food isn't buried in snow pack or beneath ice. Their nervousness translates into action. Some begin to gather into flocks, moving to staging areas where they will await some inevitable sign, some irrepressible urge, that will spur them to flight. On one of the first cool nights with a north wind, some early migrants arise from the marsh, swing around it in tight circles as if to say good-bye, spiral upward to where the winds will catch beneath their wings, and then turn and depart, not to return this year. Hardier species will tarry a bit longer, but at some point they too will find the call irresistible, perhaps even waiting until the first snow of the year slices sideways through the slough, rattling the cane and cattail with fine, hard flakes that feel like wind-driven sand. When this happens, they will rise with a wind behind them and flee the claws of grasping winter.

But when the warm winds do return, so too will the soul of the marsh, the ducks that for uncounted generations have made this place their home. The ducks' tight, quick cycle of mating, birth, and even bloody death will again return to the sloughs, with all its magic, its chores, its drama. And they will do so, again and again, as long as we conserve the places they need.

CHAPTER TWO

Fall Into Winter

Many who will read this book do not see ducks in the spring or even during what those of us who live in the North call autumn (October), but see them in the winter. The ducks arrive in warmer, southern climes like gloriously colored Christmas presents to enrich the drab months.

In the North where I live, though, ducks' autumn migration is the herald of fall, a sign that the snows will soon be on their tails, for they do not tarry once the lakes are rimmed with ice, or the first snow arrives. As wonderful as the appearance of the autumn's flights are, they bring also a sense of melancholy, for although we wait excitedly for the ducks' arrival, they pass through fleetingly, and when they depart, the world is ashen and cold, and a long winter awaits.

In many ways, ducks are lucky, for they live not just in one wonderful place

A group of ring-necked ducks lingers on a northern Wisconsin lake in late autumn.

or another, but in all of them, north and south and countless stops between. I have envied them their winged freedom, been jealous of them as they have lifted from a cold, gray lake not to return until after the ice has melted.

One need not hear a weather forecast to know that a winter storm approaches if he or she is lucky enough to be in the marsh with ducks when they feel it coming. It is an amazing thing, when you think about it, that these birds can anticipate a storm's arrival, and ride the winds that precede the storm to escape its grasp.

One day not too many years ago, I was sitting in my duck boat on a favorite lake in northern Wisconsin, with just my old and ill black Labrador, Rascal, at my side. It was early November, later than normal for a duck hunt in those parts, for ordinarily the mass of ducks would have moved through by then. But that year autumn had dawdled, and winter seemed reluctant to appear, so the bluebills and ringbills hung round this little lake, feeding on its wild rice. Rascal and I took advantage of the longer-than-usual duck season to sneak in a few extra days, for which I was thankful because this was her last autumn. I knew it, and perhaps Rascal did too, for her liver was failing from hepatitis, and I feared that with each retrieve I was perhaps seeing her last. This was a dog with whom I had traveled the flyway. Only eight years prior we had loaded the truck and followed the duck migration from Quill Lakes, Saskatchewan, to Bayou LaFourche, Louisiana, living a three-month-long waterfowler's dream. If you've had a great dog, and watched such an old friend fail, you know what I was feeling, and you know too that I'm not kidding when I say it was an honor to have spent so many fine times with her, including those last days afield.

For several days, flocks of divers had been rafted in the middle of the lake. Each time I stepped from the cabin to feel the cool night air, I had heard them out there as they ate, could hear their guttural feeding chortles. On this day, in the blackness of predawn as I set the decoys, they were still there, and later as I sat in the duck boat hidden in the rushes while first light crept over us, I watched as they grew increasingly nervous. I thought at first that their short flights were just to stretch cold wings, but gradually the small groups grew to bigger groups, and time and again they got up to wing around the lake's perimeter, only to alight again nervously in its middle. After a few such performances, I sensed there was a purpose

to this flight, and finally, though I could feel nothing in the morning except cool, still air, they rose as one, pattering first en masse across the lake, then spiraling up and up and up. I watched until they were mere black specks in the sky, for they climbed straight toward heaven, and then the mob of birds—perhaps 200 or 300—turned and headed south. They were gone, and seemingly so was every duck in the county. I saw not one more bird that day, and by nightfall a northwest wind was blowing hard. Snow dusted the ground by morning. Nights fell to near zero. Within days, the lake was frozen.

The ducks knew what they were doing.

THE MIRACLE OF MIGRATION

Not only did the ducks know what they were doing, they knew where they were going. Many, I suppose, had made this journey before, for ducks can live for 20 years, but others were still new to the world, and were for the first time traversing the continent. They likely learn migration routes in part from their elders, but it is a fact that even young ducks captured and later released without older birds to guide them have reached the wintering grounds on their own. Migration is truly a miracle, and one that, though well studied, yields almost as many questions as answers.

Not that the questions are new. We've been asking them for a long time. Humans have recorded observations on bird migrations for as long as we've had written language. In the Bible, the author of Jeremiah (8:7) wrote: "The stork in the

As long as open water remains available, many species of ducks will linger in northern areas, such as on this western river, until snow cover and colder weather drives them farther south.

©GARY R. ZAHM

heavens knoweth her appointed time; and the turtledove, and the crane, and the swallow observe the time of their coming." The Bible also tells the tale of how the Israelites, starving as they wandered through the desert of the Sinai, were saved by a flight of quail, which we now know was a fortuitous meeting of man and bird that took place as the birds migrated between their breeding grounds in eastern Europe and western Asia and their winter home in Africa. Aristotle himself wrote at length about the migrations of birds, much of which was carefully noted, although he also perpetrated a myth that some birds hibernated, a mistake that took almost 2,000 years to prove incorrect to the many who would not doubt him.

It doesn't take much brain power to deduce why ducks migrate. By moving twice a year, they can inhabit two different regions at a time when each provides favorable conditions. Ducks use the great density of small wetlands scattered throughout the North's prime breeding areas partially because the sheer number of wetlands suits their territorial behavior, and also because they can take advantage of these wetlands when they are about to produce their most abundant food crops. If waterfowl bred in winter areas, food and space resources would only support much smaller populations. It is in the best interest of the individual duck and of each species to move in the spring to places where they can flourish. In the fall, the reasons for migration are just the opposite. The ducks depart when food resources are about to decline, to gather in regions where freezing temperatures are rare and where food resources are abundant enough to sustain them during the nonbreeding season. Both weather and photoperiod stimulate this migration behavior.

How waterfowl developed this migratory tradition is still the topic of speculation, but some scientists believe these tra-

MALLARDS: ©PHOTOS-BY-RM.COM

ditions evolved after the last ice age. As the earth warmed and the glaciers retreated north, new land was exposed that was quickly pioneered by grass or tundra plant species, and on which the melted remains of these icy behemoths produced numerous potholelike wetlands. Ducks living to the south of the glaciers followed them north, generation after generation, feeding and eventually breeding in the newly created wealth of wetlands, probably pioneering into new areas as their populations grew. Eventually, they reached a latitude where in winter these wetlands would freeze, and so began filtering back south in the autumn to avoid winter's hardships. Over the ages, as the glaciers receded even farther north, the distances increased, and the longer migration patterns we see today became the norm. Or so the theory goes.

Migration—with traditions that are now quite ancient—continues to evolve as conditions change. Consider now that more canvasback winter in the Mississippi Flyway than in the Atlantic Flyway because of so much human-wrought habitat

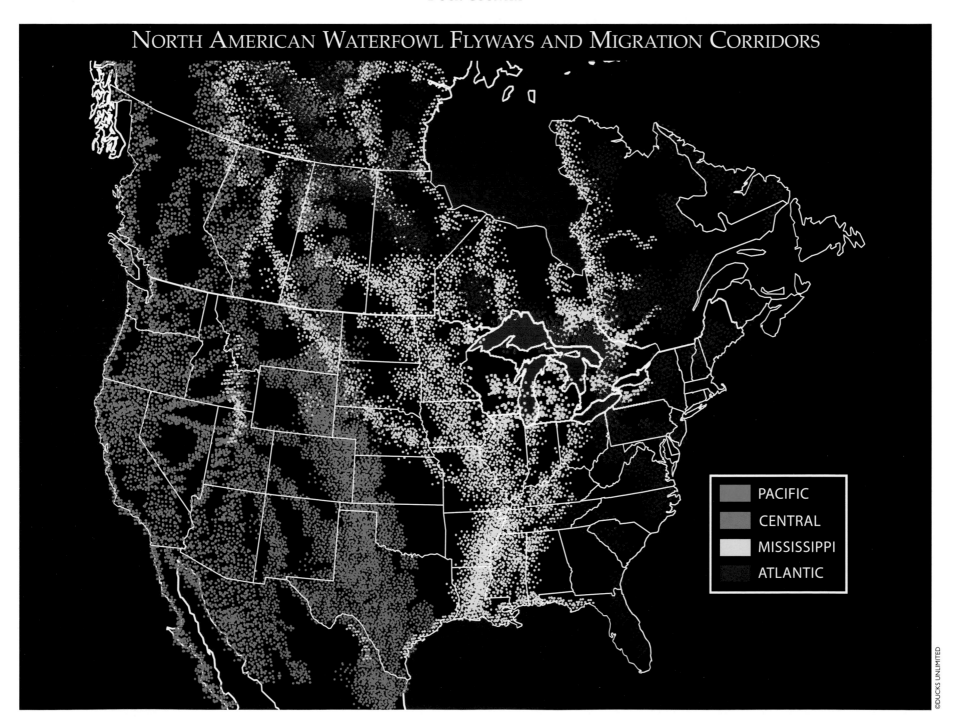

North American Waterfowl Flyways and Migration Corridors

PACIFIC
CENTRAL
MISSISSIPPI
ATLANTIC

©DUCKS UNLIMITED

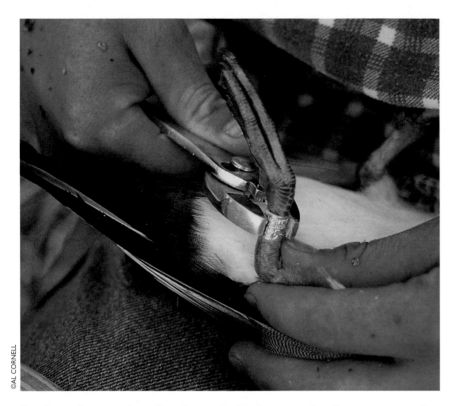

Banding information has allowed waterfowl biologists to identify migration corridors and to learn details of the migratory habits of many species of ducks.

exotic zebra mussel has proved to be a desirable food. As hurricanes rejuvenate marshes along the coast of the Gulf of Mexico, many species that would have moved on to the Yucatan peninsula have instead stayed on the U.S. side of that body of water. Forced or coerced to make changes, ducks can and do adjust, although there are limits to their adaptability.

The four flyways we've all heard so much about—Atlantic, Mississippi, Central, and Pacific—are actually more of a political arrangement for the management of waterfowl than a true map of migration. Certainly, some species—like the black ducks of the East or pintails nesting in Alaska—do indeed breed, migrate, and winter within the confines of primarily one flyway—the Atlantic for black ducks, the Pacific for many pintails. But in many cases, ducks freely move from one flyway to another. If they didn't, the coastal regions of the continent would see many fewer ducks because, as we know, the majority of dabblers nest in the Prairie Pothole Region and parklands in the center of North America. When they depart, however, while many of these prairie ducks will migrate nearly due south down the Central and Mississippi flyways, a great number will also head east or west to the perimeter flyways to spend the winter. To an even larger degree, many divers, such as ring-necked ducks, canvasback, and scaup, display this tendency to migrate east before heading south. After departing their nesting grounds in the boreal forests of northwest Canada, many divers migrate east across the trackless northern forests before dipping down to migrate north or

destruction in the latter. Mallards now often stay as far north as conditions will allow—even as far north as South Dakota—because reservoirs on rivers keep water flowing year-round, and agriculture has provided an abundance of winter foods. As long as snow doesn't cover the farm fields—so that waste grain remains available—and there is water to drink and on which to roost, mallards will stay far in the North. Bluebills are tarrying longer today in the Great Lakes during migration, and in much greater numbers than in the past, because the

©GLEN D. CHAMBERS, DU

Many waterfowl migrations take place at night. Daylight hours are reserved for resting and replenishing energy by feeding.

south of the Great Lakes on the way to their wintering grounds in the Atlantic Flyway.

These intra- and interflyway routes are called corridors, a concept pioneered by the famed waterfowl researcher Frank Bellrose, who in 1968 defined these corridors by interpreting banding data and information gleaned from airport radar equipment. More complex than the flyways, the corridors represent a better picture of the pathways down which segments

of waterfowl populations migrate. These corridors can be quite narrow, as constricted as 10 miles wide at some points. The discovery of these corridors was a significant advancement in waterfowl management because it allowed biologists to focus their attention on the protection or enhancement of important habitats within each corridor.

It may not be a great mystery why ducks migrate, but just how they navigate still remains in the realm of conjecture. There are several theories, but the fact is no one really knows how birds know where to go, and the ducks aren't talking. Certainly, one of the most important tools ducks use is their excellent vision, which can, on clear days and from an eleva-

Biologists believe ducks find their way during migration by recognizing and using a number of navigational aids, including geographical landmarks, celestial clues from star positions, and possibly even by responding to magnetic fields.

©SCOTT LILES, DU

tion, distinguish from great distances landmarks that they use as navigational clues. It is believed not only that ducks make use of the terrestrial clues below them, but also that they make use of the stars above. In one interesting study, birds were placed in a planetarium and exposed to night sky star patterns for different seasons and localities projected overhead. When shown familiar star patterns, the birds' orientation was normal, but when unfamiliar skies were projected overhead, the birds were confused and disoriented. Although these experiments were not done with ducks, it is probable that they too use the relative positions of sun and stars as aids to navigation. They may even have an internal compass that allows

them to navigate in fog or heavy clouds. Scientists probing the mysteries of migration have discovered the presence of a small amount of iron-rich tissue in the brains of some birds—tissue that seems to respond to magnetic fields much the way a compass does, a hypothesis that may be reinforced by Bellrose's studies. Using radar readings of waterfowl migrating at night between layers of clouds (they could see neither the stars nor the earth), Bellrose found that the birds' travel was still well oriented, even though they lacked landscape or celestial clues.

Unlike the story at the beginning of this chapter, in which the bluebills and ringbills departed in the morning, much waterfowl migration takes place at night. Daylight hours are spent feeding to replenish energy, and so night often is chosen as the time to migrate. But like the story just mentioned, they also will make daytime departures, especially when weather conditions are favorable, or an impending storm requires it. Occasionally, a particularly severe late autumn storm or rapidly dropping temperatures can cause mass migrations of ducks and geese, which waterfowlers call a "grand passage." During these events, millions of waterfowl will be on the move simultaneously, fleeing just in front of the change in weather, their mass departure lighting up radar screens across the Upper Midwest. Several years ago, while perched in a duck blind on a very cold morning, I was lucky enough to watch a passage of ducks that began about an hour after sunrise and took nearly two hours to parade past. Through binoculars I could see flight after flight of ducks moving due south several thousand feet above me, barely visible to the unaided eye. Quite a wonderful sight to see, but also a bit frustrating, since not a single flock dropped down to the lake where I sat. Probably they had been traveling all night, and were bound to put on some more miles before resting. Later, when checking weather reports, I learned that the marshes of Manitoba had been hard hit by record cold, prompting this mass departure of ducks.

Although these mass migrations may take ducks great distances in a short time, most migration takes place with much smaller flocks, with each species on its own timetable.

MIGRATING GREATER AND LESSER SCAUP. ©DAVID STIMAC

LESSER SCAUP: ©BILLMARCHEL.COM

Nonetheless, the speed at which they are able to migrate is impressive. Most ducks migrate at speeds of somewhere around 40 to 60 miles per hour, which allows them to cover great distances in a relatively short period of time. For instance, many blue-winged teal banded on Canadian breeding grounds and recovered in South America have covered the 2,300 to 3,000 miles in just a 30-day period. The record for this marathon goes to one young male blue-winged teal that traveled from the delta of the Athabasca River in northern Alberta to Maracaibo, Venezuela, in exactly one month, a dis-

The northward migration is more leisurely than the southward fall migration. In spring, ducks move north following the "freeze-line," lingering wherever open water and food are available.

tance of 3,800 miles—requiring an average distance of 125 miles per day!

Elevation during migration depends on weather, terrain, and the species doing the flying. Sea ducks almost always fly "on the deck"—so low in fact that they often fly around a point of land rather than just flying over it—whereas other species, like the mallard, can and do fly at enormous elevation (a mallard once struck an airplane at 21,000 feet, and a 1952 expedition to Mt. Everest found a pintail skeleton at 16,400 feet on Khumbu Glacier!). However, most migration flights probably take place at heights of less than 10,000 feet—even marvelously efficient flying machines like ducks must deal with decreasing oxygen levels and frigid temperatures at high elevations—with the bulk passing over us at 3,000 feet or less. Radar studies by Bellrose indicated fall migrants flew higher than spring migrants, and he speculated this difference was because autumn winds were favorable for southerly migration at higher altitudes, while these same winds in spring would impede northerly migration, causing the birds to fly below them.

Although most ducks seldom migrate in the precise V formation so common among geese (canvasback being one exception), and although their flock sizes vary among species, they do attain significant advantage by migrating in groups of any size. Even irregularly shaped flocks of ducks provide some mechanical advantage while flying. The ducks in the lead probably work the hardest, but are spelled occasionally as ducks to the rear replace them. Those in the rear expend less effort because they benefit from the slipstream and lift of disturbed air caused by the duck or ducks immediately in front of them. Flocking has other advantages, too. Many eyes mean more advantage at spotting foods, resting areas, or landmarks while migrating, and while on the water or ground, larger numbers of birds mean more wariness in spotting predators. The great clamor created by an entire flock of alerted, escaping ducks might also startle or confuse a predator, causing hesitation or making it difficult to focus on capturing just one bird.

The spring migration of most duck species is more protracted than their autumn journey. As winter loosens its grip, the birds follow its recession northward, just behind what meteorologists call the 32-degree isotherm. North of this moving line, which advances as winter retreats, all remains frozen. South, the wetlands are open. Because spring weather is unpredictable, this line can stall, causing the birds to wait for days or weeks for a new warm front, and it can even move southward, forcing them to retreat temporarily. Inevitably, of course, winter must give way, and as they move northward, ducks make use of the shallowest of wetlands because these warm first, and so provide abundant aquatic invertebrate foods. Wet spots that will be dry within days or weeks are often the most popular, simply because they warm up so quickly. Not only are the birds refueling for the next leg of their migration, but also they are storing nutritional reserves for the upcoming breeding season. Some of these spring migration stops are critical in importance and historically significant. The Rainwater Basin of Nebraska, because of its unique location on the prairie, hosts the majority of the continent's breeding pintail population during the spring, as well as almost all of the white-fronted geese.

DUCKS AND HUNTING

Each autumn a ritual unfolds. Men and women go afield to join with nature in the most elemental way possible—going not only to observe, but to participate in an activity as old as humankind itself. They go to hunt, and for many, this means duck hunting.

That ducks are a much-honored game bird will go without saying to many who read this book—men and women who dream of mornings in the marsh nearly every day of the year. Frequently, their lives revolve around duck hunting—in the off-season they are capturing ducks on film or on canvas, they are building wood duck houses and setting them on trees, or they are training retrievers to ensure they recover the ducks they do attempt to kill.

There are also other readers of this book who may not hunt, or may even actively frown on it. I will not use this space as a means of explaining hunting, for that would require a book itself, or for apologizing for it, for I strongly believe no apologies are required. But because ducks are hunted by more than a million Americans per year, and because hunting is one cause of duck mortality (current studies show seven times more hens die trying to nest than are killed by hunters each year), some discussion is warranted about its impacts both to duck populations and to duck conservation.

No matter how one feels about duck hunting, even a cursory glance reveals one clear thing about it: Duck hunting has generated millions of dollars for conservation, preserving habi-tat that would have otherwise long ago disappeared beneath the plow or under blacktop, or been lost to urban sprawl. To that end, duck hunting is a huge environmental plus.

Each autumn, some 1.6 million federal migratory bird hunting and conservation stamps—duck stamps to most of us—are sold in the U.S., and of that number, most—about 1.5 million—are bought by waterfowl hunters, according to the U.S. Fish and Wildlife Service. Currently at $15 per stamp, the total sales generate some $24 million annually for the conservation of wetlands and the wildlife dependent on them. Millions more are generated by state duck stamp sales, or hunting license revenues themselves, much of which is also returned to conservation of waterfowl.

Since they first went on sale in 1934, duck stamps have generated nearly $600 million that has been used to preserve almost 5 million acres of waterfowl habitat in the U.S. Many of the more than 510 national wildlife refuges have been paid for in total or in part by duck stamp money, benefiting not just ducks, but many other species of birds, mammals, fish, reptiles, and amphibians. There are about 1,150 species of birds and mammals in North America, but only 145 of these are hunted, and so the funds generated by hunting expenditures, including stamp sales, are plowed into habitat and management programs that benefit most of these other species. Further, an estimated one-third of the nation's endangered and threatened species find food or shelter in refuges preserved by duck stamp funds. People also are not immune to

Private, nonprofit wetland conservation organizations greatly benefit ducks. Since it was founded in 1937, Ducks Unlimited has contributed to the conservation of more than 9.4 million acres of wildlife habitat in North America.

The sale of duck stamps annually generates $24 million for wetlands conservation across the United States. Waterfowl hunters pay additional conservation taxes on the purchases of firearms and ammunition.

the positive impacts of this program. Refuges are increasingly popular recreational destinations for those who hike, photograph wildlife, or observe birds. Even those of us who never venture outside city limits enjoy the benefits of water purification, floodwater retention, and commercial fishery enhancements that arise from the duck stamp program's emphasis on wetland protection.

In addition to federal and state conservation efforts funded by duck stamps and license dollars, the legions of duck hunters advance environmental protection through the organizations they join. Ducks Unlimited, for instance, has raised more than $1.4 billion to date, which has contributed to the conservation

MIXED FLOCK OF SHOREBIRDS: ©MIKE KHANSA

of more than 9 million acres of wildlife habitat throughout the U.S., Canada, and Mexico. State waterfowl associations and other national groups like Delta Waterfowl all have made significant contributions to habitat conservation, benefiting not only the ducks, but also all the birds, amphibians, fish, mammals, and plants associated with those wetlands. Many private landowners who are hunters, or those who lease properties for the purpose of hunting, have further contributed to wildlife conservation by investing tremendous amounts of effort and money in preserving or enhancing habitats on their properties.

One of the most important aspects of duck hunting is that it creates an advocacy group for these species and their habi-

tats. No group of people has fought harder and longer for laws or programs that preserve wetlands and prairie habitat than have duck hunters. A less measured, but certainly very important environmental plus, is the amount of food put on the table through the act of duck hunting, or its corollary, the number of domestic animals or amount of crops that do not need to be produced. If 10 million ducks are killed by hunters, then a caloric equivalent amount of chicken, beef, or even soy protein does not need to be manufactured—the latter all coming with their own host of environmental destruction and contamination problems, and the former coming with the bonus of intact, healthy ecosystems.

In part because of the desire to provide duck populations healthy enough to sustain the demand for hunting opportunities, waterfowl management has become a highly visionary environmental program, practicing ecosystem management at a level far beyond most conservation efforts. In order to effectively manage ducks, one must preserve intact habitats, or restore degraded ones, across the face of a continent—including breeding habitat, wintering areas, and the critical migration stops between. Few conservation or environmental programs are contemplated at such an integrated scale or are delivered across such a broad geographic and political swath. Even at site level, waterfowl management means protecting or mimicking nature's complexity. For instance, one cannot solely manage the wetlands on the breeding grounds, but must also ensure there is adequate upland nesting cover or old forests with nest cavities. Studies into the types of cover favored by ground-nesting prairie ducks have spurred new data on the value of native prairie grasses and forbs. This has then increased cultivation of these plants for seed so that they can be used on nesting-ground restorations, helping to increase duck production, while at the same time returning these native plants to some of their former range, and benefiting many other dwindling wildlife populations that depend on these native grasslands.

Because of the continental scale of waterfowl management, biologists quickly grasped the importance of ecosystem management at a time when other disciplines were still struggling to define it. Waterfowl managers also realized that by

In order to ensure that harvest rates reflect the relative abundance of ducks and minimize impacts on their populations, seasons and bag limits are annually adjusted up or down, based on surveys of duck production.

WETLAND REMNANT IN AGRICULTURAL FIELD; ©GARY R. ZAHM

managing these waterfowl-related resources, they were preserving biodiversity, since few ecotypes have more diverse plant and animal communities than do wetlands. In all, the positive environmental impacts of waterfowl management, as well as social benefits such as water-quality enhancements, flow well beyond the species this work was intended to aid, and far beyond those hunters who paid for it. One particular element of this management—the North American Waterfowl Management Plan (NAWMP), which coordinates waterfowl conservation efforts across Canada, America, and Mexico—is

so visionary that it serves as a model for other conservation efforts and has significantly advanced the discipline of wildlife management. If fact, current budding conservation plans for songbirds, shorebirds, and colonial wading birds have all adopted the NAWMP model as the foundation of their strategic plans.

A very nice neighbor lady once chastised me by saying, "You duck hunters join these groups and spend money on conservation just so you can kill ducks." Frankly, I couldn't argue with her too awfully much. Although many hunters are active in conservation simply because it is the right thing to do, I'd be lying if I didn't acknowledge that having duck populations robust enough to offer good duck hunting isn't also a goal. It is a dichotomy that some will never understand, and one that those of us who do it simply accept. Although the funds generated by duck hunting are put to use in many positive ways, it is legitimate to ask whether hunting also has negative impacts on duck populations. Though this seems a simple question, arriving at an answer is complex. To simplify it mightily, the answer to whether duck hunting adversely impacts duck populations is mostly "no," but sometimes it's "yes."

In years of very good production, with a fall flight of about 100 million ducks, the total number of ducks killed by hunters can be as high as 16 million. In order to ensure that such harvest rates reflect the relative abundance of ducks and minimize impacts on populations, seasons and bag limits are annually adjusted up or down, based on surveys of duck production. Some less numerous species, like the canvasback, have been protected with no harvest allowed during more years than not. Other species, like the abundant mallard, have been restricted only in the total number, or sex, that can be killed. The system is designed to provide for duck harvest, while not adversely impacting breeding populations.

One thing about duck populations is perfectly clear: They fluctuate wildly, not because of hunting, but in spite of it. Water conditions on the breeding grounds, and the quality of the nesting habitat surrounding that water, have always been, and always will be, the key determining factors in the growth and decline of most duck species. Years of good water, and good duck production, will inevitably be followed by years of drought, during which there will be insufficient habitat for all the ducks who want to use it, and duck populations will then decline. As the old adage goes, you can't stockpile wildlife.

The boom-or-bust cycle of prairie drought and wetness is a cycle under which ducks evolved, and one under which they are designed to actually flourish, thanks to the ability to produce large amounts of young when the conditions return to normal or become exceptional. In sum, the quality of habitat—winter and summer—far outweighs hunting as the prime factor in determining total duck numbers, and the loss of, or changes to, habitat due to agriculture, pollution, and development is the real constraint on the growth of duck numbers.

Which brings us back to the issue of how much money duck hunting generates for conservation. Habitat loss is, unfortunately, a given—it continues yet, has gone on now for several centuries, and would go on at an increased rate without the slowing impacts brought about by duck hunters. Habitat conservation is not a given, and likely would advance at a much slower pace without the active participation of hunters or the hunters' dollars. As such, hunters and the ducks have forged a mutually beneficial relationship. The question isn't, at least for me, "How many more ducks would we have if none were shot each fall?" but instead, "How many fewer ducks would there be without hunters?"

©SCOTT LILES, DU

WILLOW OAK ACORNS; ©F. EUGENE HESTER

A duck's fitness, the quality of its plumage, its relative size, and its breeding potential are all, in part, determined by the quality and quantity of the bird's food. Common winter foods for some species include waste grains of commercially grown rice (above) and wild acorns (right).

54

THE ROLE OF WINTER

If summer is a time to reproduce, winter is a time to prepare for that arduous exercise. Ducks in winter are not simply loafing around on vacation. Many important breeding functions actually begin on the wintering grounds.

As discussed in the chapter on reproduction and nesting, courtship begins in winter, and pair bonding for many species occurs before they depart in spring for the nesting grounds. But there is more going on than just nuptial displays and mate selection. Where ducks go and what they eat—waste grains or natural foods—during their winter retreat can be correlated with how well they survive winter and perhaps how well they reproduce months later.

As we've seen, those ducks that are most fit tend to pair up earlier, and drakes that are most attractive and large are more successful in competing for mates. Paired ducks are higher on the social scale and have better access to food, and the female feeds more effectively because she is guarded by her drake. Thanks to pairing, fitness is further increased, as is reproductive potential. But fitness, the quality of plumage, and a bird's relative size are all, in part, determined by the quality of the duck's food. As you might guess, the quality of food is itself in part dependent on the quality of the wetland habitat. One study showed that black ducks with access to ample winter food paired earlier than those that did not. Another study indicated that mallards wintering in the bottomland hardwood forests of the lower Mississippi River val-

ley during wet winters (good habitat conditions) had higher reproductive success the next spring and summer than in years when winter habitat conditions were less favorable. This same link has been made for pintails. In a Central Valley study, pintails facing a dry winter and poorer quality foods curtailed courtship, and females delayed their winter molt, both of which may have ultimately reduced their reproductive success.

While the quality of winter habitat is important to duck reproduction, the quality of spring migration habitat is also a critical factor. While some species of ducks are efficient at storing nutrients in winter that will aid in egg laying later, many are not, and both types still depend on the fats and proteins gained during migration layovers, since these reserves are stored immediately prior to nesting.

The importance of these winter and migration habitats has become a major focus of waterfowl managers in the last two decades, prior to which much of their effort was put into understanding the northern breeding cycle. It shouldn't come as a surprise to anyone, though, that what happens to ducks and their habitats in the South plays an important role in reproduction. In fact, it would be surprising if it didn't.

On the wonderful trip during which Rascal and I followed waterfowl from Saskatchewan to Louisiana, chronicled in my book *On the Wings of a North Wind*, we had the chance to see many of these important migration and winter habitats. Wild rice lakes in Minnesota were alive with buzzing flocks of ring-necked ducks, while the pools of the Mississippi played temporary home to white-backed rafts of bull canvasback. The shallow, pothole-like wetlands of Nebraska's Rainwater Basin were dotted with thousands of pintails, the drakes beginning to show their distinctive long tails.

In the bottomland forests of Arkansas, I leaned against knotted old oaks while Rascal perched on stumps, and we watched as wood ducks and mallards flitted skillfully through the limbs of trees bereft of leaves, branches grasping like the gnarled fingers of an old woman's hands. We lay together, I on my back, on levees surrounding rice fields, and watched in wonder as mallards and pintails parachuted straight down from unimaginable heights, great wings sifting air through primaries, the rushing sound a delight, the sight of it all humbling.

Finally, we boated far out into Louisiana's coastal marshes, guided by gifted and cordial Cajuns, slept in the bayou at night in a building on stilts, only to arise to the sight of ducks by the thousands. From our pirogue, in an invisible blind woven by our skilled hosts, we watched as gadwall streaked by on a cold (for Louisiana!) wind, so low I could have batted them down with my shotgun, and saw thousands of green-winged teal slice the gray sky, flashing a semaphore of wildness over the lonely marsh.

What struck me most about being at the bottom of the funnel was just how finite the winter resources of waterfowl are. While they nest across a broad swath of the northern third of this continent, in winter they are confined to much less habitat, and this habitat is among the most threatened anywhere. I wondered, as I watched, whether we had the good sense, or the humility, to protect what is left, and to put our own needs aside once in awhile, so that the richness of wildfowl, which we have inherited, will be a legacy we can bequeath future generations.

Only time will tell.

Time is a thing with which ducks are familiar. Time to evolve over long ages, changing and specializing into myriad species. Time to fly south to escape winter. Time to fly north to reproduce. And time sitting patiently in hiding, risking all while incubating precious eggs.

All that they need to know in order to survive was taught them over time, woven into each molecule, coded in DNA. Ducks have all the tools they need to flourish, except one. They cannot undo the changes we've made to their habitats. The skills and niches they've developed mean that they cannot quickly adjust, cannot simply nest someplace else or in some other type of cover, cannot change their diet.

It is the sign of our time that skills that took millions of years to perfect may no longer suffice, thanks to the changes in habitat we've wrought in just one century. Given a chance, ducks will always prosper, but only if we acknowledge their needs, and provide for them.

If we do, then not only will the ducks benefit, but so will we all.

MALLARDS: ©STEPHEN KIRKPATRICK

Quality wintering habitat is vitally important to all waterfowl. Flooded timber in the lower Mississippi Alluvial Valley offers essential foods as well as refuge to a large portion of the continent's mallard population.

58

CHAPTER THREE

The Amazing World Of Ducks

If ducks are magic, they are nonetheless also flesh, bone, and feathers—remarkably swift fliers and beautiful to behold. They are also a wonderfully diverse group of birds. Though we tend to think of them as creatures of the North, ducks are indeed found worldwide, breeding on every continent but Antarctica. Some species—like the mallard, found across almost all of the Northern Hemisphere—enjoy huge distribution and populations, while others—like the Eaton's pintail, found only on two small islands southeast of the southern tip of Africa—are incredibly restricted in range. A few, like the Auckland Islands' flightless teal, can neither fly nor migrate. Yet others, like our own blue-winged teal, dart through the air like feathered thoughts and migrate long distances, spanning continents.

There are ducks that nest in trees, in holes in the ground, on rocky islands, and in verdant grasslands. Many ducks are tropical, sharing dank forests with mon-

Amazingly diverse birds, ducks breed in a variety of environments, including rocky coastal areas.

keys and jaguars, while others frequent the subarctic and nest near sites where giant polar bears give birth. A few eat nothing but fish and are efficient predators, nearly as swift underwater as on the wing, while still others eat almost nothing but plant matter and graze on land like geese. Ducks are found in salt water, brackish water, and freshwater, and some—the torrent ducks—live only in mountain streams where they walk or swim beneath churning white water, feeding primarily on caddis fly larvae.

In fact, it is the adaptation to narrower and narrower niches—specialized places to nest, the use of unique food resources—that helped drive the evolution of ducks toward those species we know today. There is hardly an ecosystem in the world that isn't blessed with at least one kind of duck. Despite this grand diversity, and except for the few rare oddities, ducks are remarkably more similar to each other than they are distinct.

59

By the time humans showed up in North America, its community of waterfowl had long been complete. In fact, the world was gifted with an amazing and delightful array of ducks, geese, and swans, leaving almost no region devoid of at least one representative.

THE SHAPE AND SOUND OF DUCKS

At first glance, ducks, geese, and swans may seem to be increasingly larger versions of each other. Clearly, they are related, and share many physiological similarities. But there are also many differences, the most obvious being differences in reproductive strategies and in plumage. Geese and swans form lifelong pair bonds, and both parents share brood-rearing duties, while the majority of ducks, though monogamous during any one mating season, generally choose a new mate each year, and the female raises her young alone. Geese and swans are also monomorphic—that is, males and females of the species exhibit the same plumage and are essentially visibly identical. Most ducks, however, are dimorphic, which simply means that males and females have conspicuously different plumage. Most male ducks are in fact quite gaudy, donning bright colors in autumn and winter in order to attract mates. Female ducks usually display cryptic coloration—subtle shades of browns, grays, and blacks that help camouflage them while sitting on a nest. Ducks also have two complete plumage molts per year, compared to only one for geese and swans.

A STACK OF BILLS

One of the most obvious shared traits of all waterfowl is also one or their most distinctive anatomical features—their bills. Unlike the hooked, ripping bill of raptors, or the pliers-like beaks of grosbeaks, the bills of most waterfowl are a flattened, spatulate affair, tipped with a small, shield-shaped nail called a dertrum. This nail, by the way, is used by many diving ducks as a crowbar to pry mollusks from rocks. Unlike the bills of grouse and most other birds, which are hardened (the technical term is keratinized, the same process that gives us hard fingernails), the epidermal layer of waterfowl bills is rather soft, with sensitive nerve endings along the edges that provide a sense of touch, so that waterfowl can discriminate among foods.

SURF SCOTER: ©CLIFF BEITTEL

The relatively large bills of scoters and eiders allow them to crush heavy-shelled mollusks and feed on the internal soft parts of these marine invertebrates.

Certain species, such as whistling ducks and wood ducks (above), are especially adept at perching in trees.

Though the bills of waterfowl largely look the same to us, thanks to adaptations designed to utilize different foods some specialization has occurred. The bill of the merganser, for instance, is narrow and serrated for grasping fish, while the spoon-shaped bill of the northern shoveler is a particularly flattened sieve for straining fine foods. All waterfowl have lamellae—thin, corduroy-like ridges inside the bill that act as strainers when the bill is closed and water is expelled by tongue action—which are most highly developed in the shoveler. Contrast this soft sieve with the more hardened lamellae of geese and some ducks, which serve them well for sheering grass or for stripping seeds from stems.

WORLDWIDE WEBS

Of course, the webbed feet of waterfowl are nearly as much an identifying feature as the bill. Ducks, geese, and swans all have three forward-facing toes and one short toe to the rear, each tipped with a sharp nail. The rear toe of diving ducks is fleshier than that of dabblers. Waterfowl also have scaled, leathery lower legs that are free of feathers. The legs of diving ducks are set farther back on the body than the legs of dabbling ducks and whistling ducks, so that divers, especially, are well positioned for swimming, but are rather poorly suited for walking. Because of this, their center of gravity is slightly ahead of their legs, and in order to compensate, waterfowl must maintain their balance with their toes. In addition, their broad bodies require the legs to be swung slightly outward

61

©JACK DERMID

Waterfowl use their bare legs as a means of thermoregulation. In very cold water, or when standing on ice, they can constrict the amount of blood flowing through their legs and feet, thereby preserving body heat.

CANVASBACK: ©SCOTT NIELSEN, DU

Positioned on either side of the head, the eyes of ducks allow them to see in a continuous arc of 340 degrees.

name implies, wood ducks are among several species that are quite comfortable grasping tree branches with their feet.

A duck spends more time on the water than it does in the air during the course of its life. Even newly hatched ducklings can dive or swim shortly after leaving the nest. Swimming and diving, then, are well-developed skills. Strong leg muscles drive the webbed feet backward, alternating between left and right. During the backward stroke, the web is extended fully to provide propulsion, but on the forward stroke the web is collapsed and the toes are gathered to reduce resistance. Ducks swim at an average speed of three miles per hour, but for short bursts can swim considerably faster.

All waterfowl can dive, though diving and sea ducks are better at it than most. Some ducks can even inflate or deflate their internal air sac—connected to the lungs and extending into the body cavity—to alter their buoyancy. To further aid submerging, diving ducks can even squeeze the air from their thick undercoats of down by compressing their outer plumage, an amazing feat of muscle control. While underwater, most ducks use only their feet for propulsion, which are paddled simultaneously, though the hooded and red-breasted mergansers may also flap their wings as if flying underwater. Most dives are shallow, and even diving ducks rarely descend more than 20 feet.

If those scaly, feather-free legs are rather distinctive, they are also well adapted to more than just swimming and diving. Waterfowl use these bare legs as a means of thermoregulation.

when brought forward, yielding their familiar waddling gait. Despite this, several dabblers, such as mallards and pintails, are adept at feeding on land. Diving ducks tend to be less comfortable on land since their legs are shorter and located even farther to the rear. Some species, particularly whistling ducks and some geese, have longer legs set farther forward, are proficient walkers, and stand considerably more upright. As their

In very cold water, or when standing on ice, waterfowl can constrict the amount of blood flowing to these extremities, thereby preserving body heat. Even though the body temperature will remain unchanged in cold weather (ranging from about 99 to 103 degrees Fahrenheit), the temperature of the feet will drop to just a few degrees above freezing. In the summer, waterfowl can increase the blood flow to their feet, allowing them to dissipate heat to help them stay cool.

THE EYES HAVE IT

Although you may not at first realize it, the eyes of waterfowl are extremely large relative to their body size. They appear small to us because of the lid surrounding them, but in fact they take up a considerable portion of the head. If you were to weigh the eyes of a mallard, you'd find that together they nearly equal the weight of the duck's brain.

Giving such space to eyes is no accident. Birds as a whole have the best eyesight in the vertebrate world, and it makes sense, when you stop to think about it. Clearly, excellent eyesight is a great aid for bird flight, allowing them to avoid obstructions, to spot potential foods and resting areas from great elevations, and, for those species that travel in flocks, to avoid flying into each other. How many times have you watched as a flock of teal turn in flight as if controlled by one thought? It is unlikely that they are telekinetic, though. More likely, their acute sight triggers their excellent reflexes the second they detect a flock mate changing direction.

Although the eyesight of ducks and other waterfowl may not be as acute as that of hawks or eagles, it nonetheless is superior in many ways to our own. Positioned on either side of the head, the eyes of ducks allow them to see in a continuous arc of 340 degrees—compared to our paltry 180. This means that except for a small blind spot directly behind them, waterfowl can at one time see almost the entire horizon, while simultaneously spotting a peregrine falcon directly overhead. Whereas you and I can only see something clearly when we focus both eyes on it, and then must move our eyes to the next object before we can bring it into focus, waterfowl see everything in sharp focus simultaneously, from near to far, and from left to right. Combined with excellent color vision, these attributes allow them to spot foods, or predators, efficiently. It is no wonder then why duck hunters go to such extreme lengths to camouflage themselves, and equally no wonder why those efforts frequently fail to fool waterfowl. Color vision may also help ducks discriminate between various foods, and results in, or explains the reason for, the males of many birds donning their bright hues. There would be little advantage in dressing up for the ladies if they couldn't see your bright colors.

Our eyes are superior, however, in one respect. Because our eyes are set in the front of our head, each eye's field of view overlaps, yielding binocular vision. This allows us to accurately assess both size and distance. Waterfowl have limited binocular vision, for their field of view only overlaps slightly to the front. This limited depth perception may explain why some birds hit the water rather hard when landing. It may also explain why waterfowl frequently backpeddle, in an attempt to hover, as they approach a landing—to give them time to better judge the distance. Depth perception is also an aid in selecting items—in our case, we use it to accurately pick things up with our fingers. Since waterfowl lack depth perception much beyond the tip of their bill, the sensitivity of their bill may have evolved so they can discern what they are grasping by feel. This sense of feel may also be more important for determining food choices than is their sense of taste, which is poorly developed.

MORE THAN A QUACK

Anyone who has tried to sneak up on resting waterfowl has realized that, though their vision is their most acute sense, they can hear quite well, a development typical of species that use voice communication for clues to mating and for bonding. While a bird's cochlea—the site of the sense of hearing—is but one-tenth the size of that found in comparably sized mammals, it contains 10 times the number of hair receptors. In other words, though they may hear differently than mammals do, they may be more sensitive to some sounds.

In fact, if hearing weren't important to them, waterfowl wouldn't be among the most vociferous of birds. They use a variety of calls as a means of warning each other of predators, for attracting mates, for directing and reprimanding offspring,

and for flock unity. Hen ducks are the noisiest, which makes sense when you consider their role as sole caregivers of offspring. But all waterfowl have calls—even the mute swan.

Males of almost all duck species play no role in the rearing of broods. Females, if they are to ensure the survival of ducklings, need to use their voice to guide their offspring through a dangerous world that largely considers young ducks as something good to eat. Hens use one call to disperse their young when danger appears, and another to reassemble the brood when the coast is clear. Ducklings also call to their mother to communicate their emotional or physical condition, or to locate her. This communication between hen and ducklings begins before the eggs hatch, and even the ducklings-to-be communicate with each other before emerging from the egg, a mechanism that is believed to help synchronize hatching.

Each species of duck has its own unique calls that are genetically programmed, simple, and highly understandable to others of its own species. Because each species' calls are unique, and because of distinct differences in plumage between species, these factors help to ensure that adult males and females of the same species mate together, avoiding hybridization (which still does sometimes occur). During the pairing and mating season, females of both divers and dabblers utter an incitement call, which instructs their chosen mate to attack other males. The familiar decrescendo call—the loud series of quacking notes that descend in both volume and pitch, and which hunters mimic with the highball call—is

WOOD DUCK BROOD: ©RICHARD DAY/DAYBREAK IMAGERY

uttered by female dabblers separated from their mates or from the flock, or when announcing they are willing to select a mate. While the call of most hen dabblers is a form of the familiar quack, wood ducks have a screeching *wheek whee-e-ek*, and hen diving ducks typically call with a low, harsh growling.

Although females are more vocal than males, and hen dabblers are more vocal than hen divers, males do make some vocalizations, especially when attending to females. Dabbling duck drakes typically emit a grunt-whistle call when displaying during courtship, although at very low volume. Drake divers are even quieter, and their display calls are low mewing or cooing sounds. Of course, in nature there are always exceptions. The drake redhead issues a loud meow not unlike that of a cat, the drake common eider coos loudly but soothingly, and the drake oldsquaw utters a wild yodel that can be heard for half a

RUDDY DUCK: ©BILLMARCHEL.COM

A hen wood duck communicates with her brood (above). Drake ruddy ducks perform an audible bubble display to prospective mates.

RING-NECKED DUCK: ©CATHY & GORDON ILLG

Diving ducks (above) must run on the water before attaining flight. Dabblers (below) can spring directly into the air.

NORTHERN SHOVELER: ©BRIAN WOLITSKI

mile. Even when not courting, the calls of some drakes can more accurately be called a whistle than a quack. For instance, wigeon and pintail drakes call to their mates while on the wing. The pintail drake has a flutelike whistle, while the wigeon male's vocalization is a three-note piping sound, not unlike the sound made when blowing a toy whistle with the pea removed.

The sounds that ducks make aren't completely limited to their voice calls. Wing movement during nuptial displays, and the sounds made by this movement, play a role in courting. The comical little drake ruddy duck even possesses inflatable air sacs on its throat, which he beats with his bill while courting, emitting a drumming sound.

BUILT FOR SPEED AND DISTANCE

Of all the waterfowl species, ducks are the most compact. They have comparatively massive pectoral muscles that are anchored deeply in a strong-keeled breastbone, a configuration that gives ducks their broad-chested shape. These pectoral muscles comprise, in some species, more than 30 percent of the duck's weight. Waterfowl have dark, purplish-colored, fine-grained breast muscles, the result of compounds in the flesh that carry the oxygen waterfowl need to metabolize fat, which is the fuel used for long-distance flight. These compounds are rare, are or lacking, in white-fleshed birds such as grouse, which fly only short distances. However, a grouse's white muscles contract more rapidly than the red muscles of a duck, which is why a grouse can burst more quickly into flight.

A duck's twice-a-year marathon migration requires a high metabolic rate, and its respiratory system—among the most efficient of all vertebrate species—occupies about 20 percent of the bird's volume. Even the duck's muscles aid in respiration, since they contain large amounts of respiratory structures, called mitochondria.

It is no secret to any of us who have watched a flock of ducks beat strongly into a fierce headwind that they are powerful fliers, but the same build that allows them to do just that renders them incapable of soaring—their robust build and rather short wings yield a ratio of wing surface to body weight that is among the lowest of birds that fly. Thanks to a better wing-to-weight ratio, dabbling ducks can leap directly into the air from both water and land, but the shorter-winged, heavier-bodied diving and sea ducks must first run on the water before rising. Because they can leap skyward from the ground, puddlers can and do alight on land, whereas divers are all but helpless once on the ground.

Short though a duck's wings are, they are relatively broad and well arched, and are contoured to thin leading edges, making ducks truly impressive flying machines. The arch shape is what produces lift. As air flows over the arched top of the wing, it becomes compressed, though the air beneath the wing does not. This compression causes the air over the wing to travel faster than the air below, resulting in lower air pressure beneath the wing, lifting the duck. During the downstroke of the wing, forward thrust is developed by the 10 primary feathers, which are at the trailing edge of each wing. It is this pow-

Dabbling ducks have wing patches displaying color patterns that are distinct for each species, a trait that helps ducks identify members of their own species and avoid hybridism.

erful wing stroke that allows ducks to fly into fierce winds that ground many other species of birds. It also allows them to fly swiftly. Canvasback have been clocked at more than 70 miles per hour in normal flight, and mallards at 60. Routine flight, though, is most often in the 30-mile-per-hour range.

BIRDS OF A FEATHER

It is yet another obvious characteristic of birds that they have feathers, and all waterfowl have a heavy layer of outer feathers, which are smooth, compact, and waterproof, over a thick layer of insulating down. These layers are a significant adaptation that allows them to thrive in cold climates. Waterfowl down, with its complex formation that creates dead air spaces that trap body warmth, is probably nature's best insulation, and is still used in coats and jackets because few synthetic insulators can rival it. Not only does down insulate waterfowl so that they can live in cool northern climes, but it also plays a role in reproduction. Females of most species pluck down from their own breast, placing it in their nests to surround the eggs during incubation, and even spreading it over the top of the eggs to keep them warm while they take a break to feed or drink. Down also comprises the hatchling's first coat of feathers, a warm layer that shields them from cool weather.

Swans are among the most heavily feathered of all birds, and may have more than 25,000 feathers at any given time. Compare that to the diminutive teal, which has about half that number. The total weight of a waterfowl's feathers equals about 4 to 12 percent of its body weight—that's about six pounds on a swan!

Both sexes of the dabbling duck species have bright patches on their wings called speculums, which are frequently metallic colored. Such metallic-colored plumage is rarer on diving ducks, and when found is usually limited to the head. Although divers lack speculums, they frequently have contrasting washes of white or gray on the wings' upper surface.

All waterfowl shed their flight feathers annually in a molt during which they are temporarily flightless, unlike, for instance, members of the pheasant or grouse families, which molt gradually and are never flightless. Whistling ducks, geese, and swans have but one complete molt per year, during which both their flight and body feathers are shed. Most ducks go through two sequential body molts per year, but flight feathers are shed only once. Hen ducks typically molt their flight feathers during the brood-rearing period of midsummer, whereas drakes usually molt after most females have nested or renested. Then, males may move some distance and gather in flocks called bachelor groups on large wetlands to undergo their molt. Regrowth of feathers takes about three weeks. During this period, males assume a drab coloration, sometimes called the eclipse plumage, which resembles that of the hens. They attain their distinctive nuptial plumage in fall and winter, preceding the courtship period, and retain these bright colors until the annual molt of the following summer.

Finally, ducks, as well as all other waterfowl, have a large gland above the base of the tail that secretes an oily substance for waterproofing feathers. Ducks rub their heads and bills on this spot—known as the uropygial, or preen, gland—to collect oil to distribute to the rest of their feathers. If you've ever noted how beautifully water beads up on a duck's feathers, you have some feel for the effectiveness of this substance. Even downy ducklings must preen in order to be able to float. Preening not only keeps the otherwise delicate feathers waterproof, but it also keeps them aligned and smooth for flight. Feathers are drawn gently though the bill and nibbled, realigning the vanes and restoring feather structure. Though most often done onshore, those ducks less well adapted to land preen while afloat, rolling over on their sides to reach parts of the body that would normally be submerged.

No one who has ever beheld a mallard drake in its nuptial plumage can doubt the beauty of ducks. Nor can anyone who has watched the aerobatics of ducks doubt how wonderfully they are adapted to flight. Even the homely bill of the shoveler is a wonderful adaptation, allowing it to utilize foods that other ducks cannot.

None of this is an accident. Down through the ages, nature fine-tuned ducks. Natural selection worked to strengthen species, and also created diversity, evolving new species that could adapt to habitats where as yet no duck had made a living. As time passed, the less adept succumbed to rigors and

Preening keeps a duck's feathers waterproof and also helps keep them aligned and smooth for flight.

70

MALLARDS: ©BILL VINJE

were denied the chance to pass on their genes, while the skilled and well formed survived to reproduce, enriching their race.

One might argue that not only did ducks benefit from this natural selection, but so too did those of us who admire them. Without the remarkable diversity of the duck species we see today, our world would be a less interesting place. Consider how lucky we are that so many niches were filled—one species simply couldn't fill all the voids. The most adaptable duck is probably the mallard, which numbers, in good years, about 9 million breeding birds in North America. If there were

no pintails, it isn't likely that their niche would be filled by greenheads, and we'd be out some 3 million ducks. Nor would mallards fill the niches left empty if there were no scaup, no redheads, no wood ducks. No, the specialization to use nearly every type of nesting cover, nearly every size slough, nearly every latitude, and nearly every conceivable food source has lent strength to the family of ducks, ensuring its survival. And those of us who admire them benefit nearly as much, for no matter where we live, we are blessed with the magic presence of one duck species or another.

CHAPTER FOUR
The Ducks Of North America

In the cool light of dawn, wood ducks careen through shadowed flooded timber with the grace of bats catching insects. Twisting through grasping branches, they capture our admiration as they pass.

Pintails spiral down from clear blue skies, plummeting toward a picked grainfield. Mere specks at first, as they drop their gray cupped wings and the drakes' white bellies leap into our sight. While we watch their rapid plunge and listen as air sifts through wings, that "elevator feeling" wells up in the pit of our stomach. At that moment, there is no finer place on the globe to be, no more moving sight to see.

On teeth-chattering November mornings, while we shiver in our boat hidden among the reeds, barrel-chested bluebills rip through the gray day, scouring the tops of wind-bent rushes. Surprised by their arrival, our gasps are drowned out by the roar of air torn by stubby wings,

This handsome pair of redheads is just one example of the beauty and grace that ducks lend to the wild places they frequent.

lifting our hats and our spirits. In an instant the frost is forgotten, our duck-heated blood pumped even to frozen fingers. A coiled retriever hardens with anticipation.

We are lucky, those of us who live for days in the marsh, fortunate to see and hear ducks in all their wild glory and to do so in places untamed by man. These are not the bread-fed mallards of a city park that most people know, the wallowing fakes who have traded freedom for food. Nor are we, at least temporarily, the deskbound drones of civilization, but suddenly and shortly we are one with a wildness born in dark eons past, brought to the surface by the marvel of flashing wings.

Whether you live on a sparkling ocean coast, reside in the forested Northeast, call as home the great river country of the Midwest, or ply the plains and mountains of the North American midcontinent, you are never far from the magic of ducks. We are blessed here with diving ducks, dabbling ducks, sea ducks, eiders, and even perching and whistling ducks. Few niches have gone unfilled, not even the dry Southwest, for even there, in its occasional oases, ducks come to spend the winter.

Though some duck species' numbers are now diminished compared to presettlement times, and even one lovely North American duck—the Labrador duck—is now extinct, we are still virtually surrounded by ducks of every shape, size, and color.

And that is a very good thing.

Today, the family Anatidae—in which all ducks, geese, and swans are included—contains seven subfamilies, eight tribes, 50 genera, and 162 species. Fifty-eight of those species are either geese, swans, or whistling ducks, and are found in subfamily Anserinae, while ducks, which number 104 species, are found in the subfamily Anatinae.

NORTH AMERICAN DUCKS: THE GRAND ASSEMBLY

Taxonomists further divide these subfamilies into tribes. Those ducks that most of us call puddle ducks are in the tribe Anatini. In North America, this includes the mallard (and its offshoot, the mottled duck); black duck; American wigeon; gadwall; northern shoveler; northern pintail; and cinnamon, green-winged, and blue-winged teal. It also now includes the wood duck, a puddler that used to be classified in the group known as perching ducks, or tribe Cairinini, which taxono-

mists have recently eliminated, incorporating most of its former members into the tribe Anatini.

Our diving ducks—sometimes called bay ducks, but more accurately called pochards—are in the tribe Aythyini. North American members of this group include the canvasback, redhead, the lesser and greater scaup, and the ring-necked duck.

Sea ducks (including mergansers) belong to the tribe Mergini, though not all of these ducks actually are found on salt water, as the name might imply. North America is enriched by a diverse group of sea ducks, including the bufflehead; common and Barrow's goldeneyes; harlequin duck; oldsquaw; surf, white-winged, and black scoters; and red-breasted, common, and hooded mergansers. Tribe Mergini also includes the eiders of the world, all four of which are found in North America—the common, spectacled, king, and Steller's eiders. Finally, one North American member of Mergini, the Labrador duck, has been declared extinct.

The last tribe of ducks found in North America is Oxyurini—the stiff-tailed ducks. Oxyurini is a small family with only four members worldwide, and North America can lay claim to the peculiar little ruddy duck and the masked duck.

Also included in this book are two members of the tribe Dendrocygni—North America's fulvous and the black-bellied whistling ducks. These ducks actually share many traits with geese, and in fact are classified in the same subfamily in which geese and swans are found, Anserinae.

76

DABBLING DUCKS

Tribe Anatini

Dabblers to most of us, puddlers to others, the tribe Anatini is well represented in North America with 11 species.

Whether you call them dabblers or puddlers, these ducks got their names from their proclivity to inhabit relatively shallow marshes and to feed by dabbling—that is, by tipping up on end, with head submerged. Generally associated with biologically diverse freshwater wetlands, a few species overwinter in brackish marshes or coastal bays. Most feeding is restricted to waters of about a foot in depth. Primarily crepuscular (dawn and dusk) feeders, dabblers spend most middays loafing on land near the water's edge. Omnivorous in appetite, they feed mostly on vegetable matter, but also consume invertebrates, increasing their intake especially just before and during the breeding season. Like those of all other ducks, their ducklings are precocial—that is, they can feed themselves and walk or swim almost immediately after hatching. Dabbler ducklings are carnivorous for their first few weeks, feeding almost exclusively on insects.

Although dabbling ducks can dive, particularly when pursued, their legs are situated more toward the center of the body than are those of diving ducks, which are the better swimmers. This centered leg position, however, allows dabblers to walk more easily, and because of this, several species are comfortable feeding on land. With longer wings than those of diving ducks—resulting in improvement in wing area relative to body weight—dabblers can spring directly into the air from land or water. Though they tend to be less swift in flight than diving ducks, dabblers are nonetheless fast, agile fliers.

Dabblers are gregarious ducks that frequently gather in large groups during the winter. They are also very vocal ducks, and the voice of most hens is similar to that of the well-known mallard hen's quack. Male American wigeon and northern pintail emit whistles, especially while in flight.

Most dabblers are exceedingly dimorphic in plumage—males and females differ greatly, especially during the breeding season. Notable exceptions in North America are the American black duck and mottled ducks, in which the sexes are essentially identical in plumage. Generally, dabblers undergo two annual molts of body feathers, one of which is called a prebasic molt, which occurs near the end of the breeding season and includes the shedding of wing feathers, leaving the ducks flightless. At this time, males assume drab, camouflaged plumage similar to the female, which may help hide them while they are unable to fly. This eclipse plumage is worn for two or three months. The adults of both sexes have iridescent speculums on their wings, with the exception of the gadwall.

Dabblers reach sexual maturity by one year of age, and although they nest in many regions, most nesting occurs in the North and winters are spent in the South, resulting in long migrations. Females are highly philopatric, which means they return to the place where they were hatched and previously bred. Since pair bonding generally occurs on the wintering grounds, males are not philopatric, but follow their mate to her home region. Dabblers nest primarily on the ground, frequently on uplands in heavy grass or under brush, at distances from water that may exceed a mile. They are territorial during the breeding period, attempting to exclude members of their own species from the nesting site. Males do not assist in incubation or brood rearing, but do defend their mate from rivals until she initiates incubation, after which the male departs to undergo his molt. Pair bonds last only one breeding season.

Nests are shallow, and are made of nearby vegetation and lined with down from the hen's breast. Clutches are relatively large—a dozen or so eggs are laid and incubated for 21 to 25 days, depending upon the species. Persistent renesters, many dabblers will lay a second, third, fourth, fifth, and even a sixth clutch if the previous attempts were destroyed. Downy ducklings are generally yellow buff underneath, tending toward brown black along the back and top of the head, with a dark eye stripe. Northern pintail ducklings tend more toward gray.

As with other dabblers, this mallard hen (above) handles the brood rearing on her own. After the hens have nested, drakes such as this cinnamon teal head off on their own to molt.

MALLARD PAIR. ©BILLMARCHEL.COM

MALLARD

Anas playtrhynchos playtrhynchos
Common Names: Mallard,
Greenhead (drakes), Susies (hens)
Average length—24 inches
Average weight—2.75 pounds

With a distribution that spans the northern regions of the world, the mallard is most likely the best-known duck, as well as the most numerous. In North America, in years of good water and production, mallards number about 9 million birds. The mallard is also the progenitor for most domesticated ducks, and may have been domesticated even before the chicken.

The drake's unmistakable glossy blue green head with its white neck ring gives it its common name, greenhead. The drake has a chestnut-colored breast, abruptly ending at its silver sides and underbelly, a feature readily discernible even in flight. A rim of white-edged tail feathers on the rump of both sexes is also distinct, as is the white-edged purplish blue speculum. The back is gray, the bill greenish yellow, and the legs orange or red.

The female has cryptic camouflage coloration that is mottled brown. Her head is a darker brown on top and light brown on the cheeks, and has a dark stripe that runs through the eye. The hen's bill is mottled orange, as are her legs. She shares the male's white-edged, iridescent blue speculum. Young and males in eclipse plumage resemble the female.

RANGE AND MIGRATION

In North America, the mallards breed regularly from the mid-latitude states north to Alaska, but are most numerous west of the Mississippi and Hudson Bay. Historically, the highest concentrations occurred in southern portions of Saskatchewan, Manitoba, and Alberta. These are also, however, the areas of highest recent mallard declines, the result of habitat loss caused by agriculture. In all, the Prairie Pothole

Region (including the adjacent prairie parklands) generally sees about 60 percent of the mallard breeding population. Thirty percent nest north of those areas, with the remainder scattered throughout North America, including as far south as Texas. Mallards are the most adaptable of ducks.

Mallards winter in all four flyways, often migrating no farther south than they must in order to find open water and food in the form of waste grain in agricultural fields. They will winter as far north as Montana as long as snow does not cover the farm fields. Often, the fall flight doesn't depart the prairie region until November. The Mississippi Flyway—where flooded bottomland forests are a particularly important but

MALLARDS: ©SCOTT NIELSEN, CU

Mallard hen and brood. Note that the almost fully-fledged ducklings are now nearly indistinguishable from their mother in appearance.

disappearing habitat—winters more mallards than any other. Significant numbers of mallards winter in the Pacific Flyway's Central Valley of California, as well as in the Central Flyway, particularly on the Missouri and Platte rivers, and in the playa lakes of Texas. A smaller but growing number of mallards winter in the Atlantic Flyway.

In spring, mallards (along with northern pintails) are the earliest to depart the wintering grounds, beginning in February. The first mallards arrive in the U.S. portion of the Prairie Pothole Region in mid- to late March, and, in many years, by early April they have reached the Canadian provinces.

BREEDING BIOLOGY

Mallards begin to form pair bonds as early as September, but most bonding occurs in October and November, and by January the majority of hens are found with mates. Competition for mates can lead to vigorous fighting between males. Larger and more beautifully plumed males seem to be chosen most by females. Males provide protection for females from the unwanted advances of other males, which allows the hen to feed more efficiently and to store the nutrient reserves needed for the rigors of nesting. Mallards nest in a greater range of habitats than any other puddle duck, and will even nest in artificial nesting structures. Most mallards settle in the Prairie Pothole and parkland regions first, but if drought conditions occur, will move farther north or east into forested areas to nest.

Pairs disperse to small bodies of water and establish a territory, with spacing between pairs. Territories are defended against other mallards, and the size of territories diminishes where mallard numbers are greatest. Most hens choose to nest in dense upland vegetation and under woody shrubs, and prefer overhead cover up to two feet in height. Nests are on the ground, usually within 100 yards of water and made of nearby vegetation. Once she begins to lay her eggs, down pulled from the hen's breast supplements the vegetation. She lays one gray green egg per day, generally in the morning, until the clutch—which averages nine—is complete. If the clutch is lost early in the nesting season, mallard hens will renest, though the number of eggs declines. After 23 to 25 days, the eggs hatch synchronously. The drake plays no role in incubation, and abandons the hen shortly after she begins incubating.

Usually within 12 hours of hatching, the hen leads the down-covered ducklings to a nearby wetland, where they immediately swim and learn to feed on invertebrates. The down is retained for 18 days. During their seventh week, the ducklings are covered with feathers, and can fly sometime during their eighth or ninth week.

83

AMERICAN BLACK DUCK PAIR: ©JACK MILLS

The most prized duck among eastern duck hunters, the American black duck is known for its wariness. Since it is a very close relative of the mallard, hybridization and/or competition between the two may be partially responsible for the decline of this bird as mallards move eastward in range.

Similar in size and shape to the mallard, the black duck resembles the mallard hen, although it is considerably darker. Unlike the mallard, both sexes of the black duck are nearly identical in plumage, which tends toward brown black, with a contrasting lighter brown head. The speculum of the black duck is darker than

AMERICAN BLACK DUCK

Anas rubripes

Common Names:

Black mallard, red leg, dusky duck

Average length—24 inches

Average weight—2.75 pounds

that of the mallard, and is more violet compared to the mallard's blue. The speculum also lacks, or nearly lacks, the white edges found on the mallard. The black duck also lacks the white tail feathers found on both sexes of mallards. The nearly white underwings signal a bright contrast to the dark body during flight. The voice of the black duck is identical to the mallard's.

The bill of the adult black duck drake is bright yellow, while that of the female is olive green with black mottling. Immature drakes also have an olive green bill, but it lacks the mottling. Both sexes have red legs.

RANGE AND MIGRATION

Black ducks nest in low densities across a broad range in eastern North America, from as far south as Cape Hatteras, North Carolina, north to the northern edge of the boreal forest, and west through Ontario and Minnesota. During the breeding season, black ducks inhabit freshwater and coastal marshes, as well as beaver ponds, river estuaries and floodplains, and thousands of scattered boreal lakes. They tend to use saltwater habitats more than the mallard.

In winter, black ducks migrate south as far as Florida and Alabama. Those birds from the western part of the breeding range winter in the Mississippi Flyway (about 28 percent), but by far the greater number of black ducks are found in the Atlantic Flyway's wintering grounds, with the largest concentration occurring in New Jersey. Tennessee is the most important winter destination of the Mississippi Flyway's black ducks. Like its relative the mallard, the black duck is very cold tolerant, and many tend to stay as far north as possible, given open water and food.

Since many black ducks winter in areas not far from where they breed, migrations tend to be short. Although they can often gather in large rafts on open water, in flight black ducks tend to travel in small groups of fewer than two dozen birds.

In spring, black ducks begin moving north in February, and are generally in their breeding grounds by mid-April to early May, depending on ice-out.

BREEDING BIOLOGY

Black ducks form pair ponds as early as September, and the majority are paired by December. Upon return to the nest site, drakes remain with the hen until an average of 14 days after the beginning of incubation, during which time the male defends the female from unwanted advances by other males. Because of the relative infertility of these eastern and northern wetlands (compared to prairie potholes), nest density is much lower, and home ranges can be as large as five square miles.

Hen black ducks nest in uplands most of the time, but will nest within marshes as well. Nest sites are often in forests, where the nests are built with an eye to providing overhead cover—under shrubs or blueberry bushes, beneath conifers, or in growths of nettle. Black ducks will also nest on muskrat houses or on stumps. Wooded islands are a favorite site.

Hens lay an average of nine eggs, one egg per day. Incubation periods vary, but range from 23 to 29 days. Egg laying can commence as early as mid-March or as late as mid-June, but the peak periods are the third and fourth weeks of April. Some studies show that about a third of hens that have lost their first clutch will renest, and that the clutch size will be smaller than the first.

After hatching, the ducklings are led by the hen to the nearest body of water, which can be as far as a mile away. She will remain with them until they can fly, about 60 days after hatching.

MOTTLED DUCK PAIR: ©MARIE READ

MOTTLED DUCKS

Anas fuligula (Florida Duck)
Anas maculosa (Gulf Mottled Duck)
Common Name: Florida mallard
Average length—23 inches
Average weight—2.5 pounds

Also close relatives of the mallard, the two species of mottled duck are very similar, and are distinguished largely by their geographic range: The Florida mottled duck lives, as its name implies, in the southern half of that state; the gulf mottled duck ranges from Mobile Bay, Alabama, south and west to Laguna de Tamiahua, Mexico.

Both sexes of mottled ducks resemble the female mallard, though like the black duck they are darker with paler heads. The neck is longer than that of the mallard. Breast feathers are more intensely mottled black than the mallard, hence its name, and the tail coverts and tail are darker than the mallard. The Florida drake's bill is bright yellow with a black nail; the hen's is dull orange with black spots on the saddle. The gulf mottled duck drake's bill is olive green, while the hen's bill is orange with dark spots. Usually, the white edging along the speculum is not present, and the speculum's color tends more toward green than either the mallard or black duck.

A third, similar bird, the Mexican duck (*Anas platyrhynchos diazi*), used to be considered a distinct species, but its taxonomic status is now in question due to hybridization with mallards. Darker than either the mallard or the mottled duck, but lighter than the black duck, this slightly smaller relative of the mallard is limited to the Rio Grande and Pecos river valleys of New Mexico, and adjacent Arizona and west Texas. It is also found in the mountains of Mexico.

RANGE AND MIGRATION

Florida mottled ducks live south of Tampa, and are found in freshwater emergent wetlands, wet prairies, ditches, and seasonally flooded marshes associated with major rivers. The fall population of Florida mottled ducks fluctuates, but recently has been about 60,000 birds, while the gulf population may number 100,000.

The gulf population of mottled ducks uses fresh to brackish ponds of coastal marshes, rice fields, and emergent wetlands associated with gulf coast prairies. The highest density of breeding pairs of either group of mottled ducks appears to occur in coastal Louisiana and southeastern Texas. A third

population of mottled ducks was introduced near Santee Delta Wildlife Management Area in South Carolina and is not established.

Both mottled ducks are essentially nonmigratory, though they do make some shifts up to 200 miles within their range. They rarely gather in large flocks.

BREEDING BIOLOGY

Mottled ducks breed at one year of age, produce only one brood per year, and may renest up to five times if nests are destroyed. Pair formation begins in October and is largely complete by October, which is much earlier than most other ducks. Although peak nesting occurs in March and early April, it has been recorded as early as January and as late as August.

Nests are built in dense grass or beneath brush near either freshwater or brackish ponds. An average of 10 eggs are laid, and incubation lasts about 25 days.

Some biologists have reported seeing male mottled ducks in the company of broods, leading them to speculate that perhaps mottled ducks have long-term pair bonds that last in excess of two nesting seasons. Since they are a resident, nonmigratory species, the potential exists for long-term pair bonds to occur, which would make mottled ducks unique in comparison to the closely related mallard and black duck, which exhibit only seasonal or short-term pair bonds.

PINTAIL PAIR: ©GARY R. ZAHM

NORTHERN PINTAIL

Anas acuta
Common Names: Sprig, spiketail
Average length—26 inches
Average weight—1.75 pounds

One of the world's most elegant ducks, the northern pintail is also one of the most numerous, and is found circumpolar. In North America, pintails have a larger breeding distribution than any other duck except the mallard, and no dabbling duck frequents the Arctic regions more often than this slender bird.

Pintails are graceful and swift fliers, and often plummet from great heights. They walk easily and are comfortable feeding on land. Although a drake pintail is three or four inches longer than a mallard drake, he weighs one-fifth less. The two long, black, central tail feathers on the drake in nuptial plumage amount to one-fourth of his total length. Pintails of both sexes have longer, narrower wings than other dabblers, as well as longer necks, adding to their graceful appearance. The female wears the cryptic tan and brown colors of other dabbler hens, while the male has a striking chocolate brown head and a white underbody that extends stripe-like nearly to the eye. The bill of both sexes is blue gray; the hen's

is mottled with black. The feet and legs are also gray. The hen pintail's speculum is a noniridescent brown or brown green, while the male's is a metallic green or green black. The speculum of both sexes has a trailing edge of white.

Hens have a coarser quack than a mallard, while the drake whistles.

RANGE AND MIGRATION

Pintails nest across a broad section of North America, with the highest concentrations in the Prairie Pothole and prairie parkland regions, followed by Alaska. Numbers by region fluctuate more widely than other dabblers, dependent on water conditions. In years of drought on the prairie, from 40 to 60 percent of all breeding pintails will move north to Alaska where, in more normal years, about 20 to 25 percent would be found. Some will even continue on to Siberia. This tendency to overfly the prairies when they are dry is stronger in pintails than in other ducks. Disjunct breeding populations are also found near the marshes of the Great Salt Lake, the Nebraska Sandhills, the plains of Wyoming, central California, western Minnesota, and Idaho. Few are found in the eastern half of the continent, but some small breeding populations do exist.

Pintails vie with mallards to be the earliest spring migrants, leaving the wintering grounds as early as late January, and arriving on the prairies in early to mid-April. Pintails are also among the first to migrate in autumn, depart-

PINTAILS IN COURTSHIP FLIGHT: ©BILLMARCHEL.COM

Spring courtship flights are not only visually spectacular feats of aerial acrobatics, they also help hens in identifying and selecting the strongest, most experienced male breeders. Choosing the right male is imperative to hen nesting success.

ing Alaska in August and September. Some pintails show up on the wintering grounds as early as September.

North America's pintail population winters as far south as Colombia and Cuba. Over half, however, will head to California, where they use the marshes of the Sacramento, San Joaquin, and Imperial valleys, as well as the delta marshes near San Francisco. Significant populations winter in Mexico, the interior intermountain region of the U.S., the gulf and panhandle of Texas, and the coastal region of Louisiana. A small number winter in the Atlantic Flyway in the coastal marshes of the Carolinas. Wintering pintails are not adverse to salt water, and are common on brackish marshes and lagoons. In the winter, pintails often gather in huge flocks numbering tens of thousands. Waste grain is a favorite food of wintering and migrating pintails, and they will fly 30 miles per day from roosting areas to feed.

BREEDING BIOLOGY

Nesting pintails prefer sparsely vegetated prairie, or prairie-like habitats such as pastures, and frequently choose nest sites in agricultural fields. In the subarctic or other nonprairie regions, pintails choose a variety of places as nest sites. They will commonly make nomadic migrations in search of favorable water conditions if their primary breeding habitat is dry. Pintail pairs prefer ephemeral, temporary, or seasonal wetlands to those that are more permanent, and these shallow wetlands provide animal foods important to prelaying and laying hens.

Their tendency to nest in stubble fields makes them particularly susceptible to nest destruction and hen loss from agricultural practices. One study showed that 49 percent of pintail nests in North Dakota were destroyed by agricultural activity.

Pintail hens nest at 10 to 11 months of age, and nests are often located farther from water than those of other dabblers. Because of the broad range of habitats and latitudes at which they nest, breeding times are varied, but in their primary prairie habitats, breeding begins in early April. Pair bonds form in the winter or early in the northward migration. Drakes are promiscuous, and broods may not be sired by the male of mated pairs. Once eggs are laid, drakes pursue hens of other pairs, which tends to space females apart. Hens scrape out a nest, sometimes on bare earth, and lay eggs in the morning at a rate of one per day. The average clutch is about seven eggs, and incubation lasts 21 to 23 days. Hens renest if the first clutch is lost.

In the subarctic, renesting is less common because the nesting season begins later, and the short season would not allow sufficient time for the ducklings to mature before autumn. Longer day lengths, however, allow subarctic pintail ducklings to feed during the full 24 hours of daylight, speeding growth. Subarctic pintail ducklings can fly at about six weeks of age, while lower latitude pintail ducklings, because of shorter feeding days, mature more slowly, and require seven or eight weeks to attain flight. During its first 50 days of life, animal foods make up two-thirds of a pintail duckling's diet.

AMERICAN WIGEON PAIR: ©CATHY & GORDON ILLG

AMERICAN WIGEON

Anas americana
Common Name: Baldpate
Average length—21 inches
Average weight—1.75 pounds

The American wigeon is one of three wigeon species worldwide. It is a handsome, medium-sized dabbler with narrow wings, a wedge-shaped tail, and a short bill. They are vocal ducks and quick to detect danger. Only the teal fly more erratically than wigeon, whose flock flight pattern has been compared to pigeons. Not one for great heights, the wigeon frequently flies in small irregularly shaped flocks at low elevation, even during migration. Drakes emit a three-note whistling call, of which the middle note is higher than the other two.

Wigeon are comfortable on land, where they frequently graze on succulent parts of grasses or clovers. They do not feed as selectively on the seeds of aquatic plants, as do other dabbling ducks, but

AMERICAN WIGEON AND BLUE-WINGED TEAL. ©DU

instead prefer the stems and leafy parts of pondweed, coontail, and wild celery in freshwater marshes. In coastal estuaries, they feed on eelgrass, wigeon grass, and bushy pondweed. Poor divers, they are well known for pilfering wild celery and other deep-growing plants from canvasback, coots, or other efficient divers when these birds return to the surface.

Wigeon have a bright white belly, and the males have a white wing shoulder, both of which are distinctive, even in flight. Both sexes have a salt-and-pepper pattern to the neck,

but the mature male's head sports a metallic green patch that extends from just in front of the eye to the neck. In full nuptial plumage, the top of the drake's head and its forehead are nearly white, which gives the bird its common name of baldpate—as if its "hair" were receding. Their bills are bluish, tipped with black, and their legs and feet are blue gray.

The drake's white shoulder patch is followed by a black band, then a metallic green black speculum. The hen's shoulder patch is less distinct, tending toward gray. Her speculum is black. The speculum of both sexes is bordered with white on the edge nearest the body.

RANGE AND MIGRATION

Wigeon are among the most northerly nesting of dabbling ducks, second only to pintails in abundance in the subarctic regions. The highest densities are found at Old Crow Flats and the Mackenzie River Delta, Yukon Flats, and large river deltas between Great Slave Lake and Lake Winnipeg. About one-third of the breeding population is found in the prairie parklands/Prairie Pothole Region. The intermountain valleys of the Great Basin and British Columbia also support breeding wigeon. Minnesota is the farthest east of any significant breeding population, though small numbers nest in Quebec and New Brunswick.

Most wigeon winter in the Mississippi and Pacific flyways. In the latter, the region of most importance is California's Central Valley. In the Mississippi Flyway, wigeon winter primarily on the coastal marshes of Louisiana. In the Central Flyway, the Texas gulf coast and the southern high plains are important wintering areas. Fairly large numbers of wigeon winter on the east gulf coast of Mexico, and as far south as the Yucatan peninsula. The Atlantic Flyway sees the fewest wigeon, and here they winter in coastal marshes from Connecticut to Florida.

Only the blue-winged teal and pintails migrate south earlier than wigeon, which leave the northern plains by mid-October. Subarctic-nesting wigeon depart beginning in early September. They begin to arrive on the winter areas in early October, and have largely arrived by December.

Although early to depart come autumn, they are tardy migrators in the spring, filtering north in dribs and drabs, generally arriving later than other dabblers. Pairing mostly occurs during winter, but some females arrive at their nesting grounds unpaired, where they then find mates.

BREEDING BIOLOGY

Wigeon prefer semipermanent and permanent wetlands surrounded by good upland cover, and often nest beneath brush or woody shrubs. Most nests are within 50 yards of water. As do other dabblers, wigeon hens build shallow nests of surrounding vegetation, supplemented with down from their breasts. Wigeon lay, on average, eight eggs, which take from 23 to 25 days to incubate. Males depart shortly after egg laying begins, and move to large wetlands to molt.

Wigeon broods are more sedentary than those of other ducks, and prefer larger wetlands to smaller ones. Hens remain with the ducklings until they are nearly ready to fly. Even though wigeon arrive on the nesting grounds later than mallards and pintails, and lay eggs up to two weeks later than mallards, their ducklings seem to mature more rapidly during the late stages of development, for they attain flight earlier than mallards.

GADWALL PAIR:©GARY KRAMER

GADWALL

Anas strepera
Common Names: Gray duck, gray mallard
Average length—21 inches
Average weight—2 pounds

Like mallards, pintails, and shovelers, gadwall are holarctic in distribution, found throughout much of the Northern Hemisphere. Unlike many other duck species, the gadwall is flourishing.

The gadwall is a medium-sized dabbler with wings slightly narrower than those of a mallard, and both sexes are similar in color, though not identical. In flight, the wings of a gadwall show less white than those of a wigeon, with the white toward the rear of the wings instead of the front, as on the wigeon. They appear slimmer than a mallard in flight, but not as slim as the pintail. Like the wigeon, the gadwall's white belly contrasts sharply with a dark chest. Hens quack like a mallard, but softer, while drakes whistle and emit a *geck-geck* vocalization.

Hen gadwall sport feathers typical of dabblers—straw and brown colors in a camouflaging pattern. Males tend to be grayer, with breast feathers of alternating white and black crescent lines. Gadwall bills are narrower than those of mallards, and the hen's bill is yellow, mottled with black spots. The male's bill is gray black. They have steep foreheads, and males have distinctive black humps for crowns. Unlike other dabblers, gadwall lack metallic speculums, and instead both sexes display a white speculum quite visible in flight. It is bordered to the front by black, and the drake has a rusty chestnut patch forward of this, extending to the "wrist" of the wing.

Like the wigeon, the gadwall feeds on the succulent parts of aquatic plants—more than on the seeds—and on algae, and the two species are often seen feeding together. Unlike the wigeon, gadwall are not common on land.

RANGE AND MIGRATION

Gadwall breed primarily in the Prairie Pothole Region and prairie parklands of north central North America, with just over one-third of the continental population found in the prairies of the Dakotas and southern Saskatchewan. Outside the primary prairie breeding range, gadwall also occur in significant numbers in the intermountain region, particularly in the marshes surrounding the Great Salt Lake.

Not cold-hardy birds, gadwall begin to leave the Canadian provinces in September, but usually fly a short distance south to the U.S. portion of the Prairie Pothole Region, where they will remain until the first ice in mid-October. Although the majority of gadwall nest in the Central Flyway, most gadwall migrate through the Dakotas, Nebraska, and central Kansas to the southern end of the Mississippi Flyway to spend the winter. Louisiana is home to more than 75 percent of the wintering gadwall population. Each of the other three flyways sees some gadwall in winter, but in much smaller numbers. Some winter along the east coast of Mexico, and as far south as the Yucatan peninsula.

In the spring, gadwall are among the last to arrive on the breeding grounds.

BREEDING BIOLOGY

Most gadwall breed in their first year, and pairing begins in early fall. Hen gadwall are among the last waterfowl to nest, typically in early to mid-June, long after mallards and pintails have laid their eggs. They frequently wait three or four weeks after arrival to initiate nesting. Nests are typical dabbler affairs, and the hen lays an average of 10 eggs, which she incubates for about 25 days. Duration of pair bonds is variable, but most drakes abandon their hen about two weeks into the incubation period.

Gadwall ducklings reach flying stage in about 50 days, and broods are highly mobile. Hens tend to take broods to larger, semipermanent or permanent wetlands. Ducklings switch to vegetable foods at three weeks of age—much earlier than other dabblers. Gadwall have larger brood sizes than other ducks that lay about the same number of eggs, which indicates better survival rates of ducklings. Their propensity to brood on larger wetlands, where land-based predators are less numerous, and to seek brackish wetlands where mink—major duckling predators—are rare, may be responsible for their high brood survival rates.

BLUE-WINGED TEAL PAIR. ©JACK DERMID

This small dabbler is known for its twisting, turning flight, and for flying low over marshes. The ducks' small size and rapid wing beats give the illusion of high speeds. The pale blue patches on the forewing gives this lovely bird its name. It is the third-most numerous duck in North America, the only continent on which it breeds. It migrates the longest distances of any of our ducks, wintering as far south as Peru. The Atlantic blue-winged teal (*A.d. orphana*), a slightly larger version that breeds

BLUE-WINGED TEAL

Anas discors
Common Names: Bluewing, summer teal, white-faced teal
Average length—16 inches
Average weight—15 ounces

on the northern Atlantic seaboard, is recognized by some taxonomists as a subspecies.

The pale shoulder patch is distinguishing, even in flight, and is shared by both sexes, though the female's is less distinct. Cinnamon teal and northern shovelers also have a similar blue wing patch, but the two teal rarely inhabit the same areas of the continent, and the shoveler's large bill is distinguishable even in flight.

Among the last to attain its nuptial plumage, the male

FEEDING BLUE-WINGED TEAL AND TRI-COLORED HERON: ©KIRKPATRICKWILDLIFE.COM

blue-winged teal lacks its distinctive white facial crescent in the autumn, but gains it in late November or December and sports it through the winter. In this plumage, the male also has a steel blue head and a tan chest and sides dotted with deep brown spots. Females resemble all other hen dabblers, though they are appreciably smaller and are virtually indistinguishable from hen cinnamon teal. Both sexes of blue-winged teal have dark blue black bills nearly as long as their heads, and pale yellow legs. Males have an iridescent green speculum that is separated from the blue wing shoulder with a white stripe. This stripe is lacking in the hen, and her speculum is almost black.

Blue-winged teal are more vocal than most ducks, and the hen's quacking is more rapid and softer than the mallard's; the drake has a low whistled peep.

RANGE AND MIGRATION

Blue-winged teal breed primarily in the grasslands of the Prairie Pothole Region, and in the parklands, though they also range east in significant numbers through Minnesota, Wisconsin, and Michigan, and south to Iowa and Nebraska. Appreciable numbers also nest in the intermountain region of the U.S. and Canadian west. Of all ducks, the blue-winged teal shows the least tendency to home to its natal site, and in many years they stop in areas outside their primary breeding range to take advantage of better conditions. Though some fly north to the closed boreal forest, few fly farther north than that. In some wet years a few may breed even in the coastal wetlands of Louisiana and Texas.

The autumn migration of blue-winged teal is complex, with some flying due east from the prairies before heading south. In late summer, immature blue-winged teal from the Dakotas and Montana move north into prairie Canada before beginning their southward migration. They tend to remain north into October, although portions of the population show up in the southern U.S. in significant numbers as early as September.

Although some blue-winged teal winter in the southern extremes of the three easternmost flyways, essentially none winter in the Pacific Flyway, and by far the greatest number winter outside the U.S.—from Mexico to Peru. Those that depart due east from the prairies turn south at the Maritimes, eventually to cross the Atlantic on their way to the West Indies and South America. A great number exit the prairie diagonally east through Minnesota in a straight line through Florida, then on across to South America. Another significant corridor leads through the Dakotas and Nebraska, and eventually through southeast Texas and Louisiana.

In spring, they reverse direction and begin to leave South America in February, and reach the nesting grounds on the American prairies in late March or early April, and the Canadian provinces from late April to mid-May.

BREEDING BIOLOGY

Courtship begins in the winter as the drake attains his nuptial plumage, and continues during the northward migration. By the time blue-winged teal reach the nesting grounds, most hens are paired. The pair bond is apparently very strong, and the drake stays with his hen into the third week of incubation.

Blue-winged teal are among the last dabbling ducks to nest, with a median date of May 28. Unlike gadwall, which arrive and then wait three weeks before nesting, blue-winged teal nest soon after arriving. Males tend to pursue intruding males less frequently than do drakes of other dabblers, hence they have smaller home ranges. Hens seek out grasslands for nest sites most often near small to medium-sized shallow wetlands, or the margins of larger wetlands. In addition to tall grass, the hen sometimes also favors nest sites below brush, where she builds a typical dabbler nest. Laying an average of 10 eggs, she incubates them for about 21 days.

Although blue-winged teal nest success varies according to location and habitat quality, a high brood survival rate helps offset those losses. Once the brood has reached a suitable wetland, they tend to be more sedentary than broods of other ducks, reducing the amount of overland travel to other wetlands, which may help explain the high brood survival rate. Blue-winged teal fledge—achieve flight—at about 40 days.

CINNAMON TEAL PAIR: ©GARY KRAMER

CINNAMON TEAL

Anas cyanoptera septentrionalium
Common Names: Red teal, red-breasted teal
Average length—16 inches
Average weight—15 ounces

In its nuptial plumage, few ducks are as striking as the drake cinnamon teal. His cinnamon belly, chest, and head in contrast with the bright blue forewing and iridescent green speculum are stunning, even on the wing, making the drake of this species one of the easiest to identify. The hen, however, lacks these brilliant colors, and is indistinguishable in the field from the hen blue-winged teal. The drake cinnamon teal also has distinctive red eyes, which he attains at the early age of two months. The bill is black, and feet and legs are yellow. Like the blue-winged teal, drake cinnamon teal attain nuptial plumage in winter, and throughout the summer and much of the fall the drakes are in drab eclipse plumage.

The cinnamon teal is ecologically similar to the blue-winged teal, taking the latter's place west of the Prairie Pothole Region. Because of the relative scarcity of wetland habitat in that western region, compared with the prairies, the population of cinnamon teal is much smaller. It has a similar voice to the blue-winged teal. The drake emits a low, whistled peep, while the hen quacks a soft, harsh *karr, karr, karr*. Cinnamon teal tend to fly in very small flocks of only three to five birds, and display the same quick, twisting, low-altitude flight of the blue-winged teal.

There are five races of cinnamon teal in the New World, four of which nest solely in South America, and one in North America.

RANGE AND MIGRATION

Confined largely to the western U.S., many cinnamon teal breed in Utah in the marshes of the Great Salt Lake. Cinnamon teal also breed in Oregon, California, Washington, Nevada, Wyoming, Colorado, and western Montana. Only rarely does this bird range into the Prairie Pothole Region. North of the U.S. border, cinnamon teal breed in southern British Columbia.

Like the blue-winged teal, the cinnamon teal departs the breeding grounds in late summer or early fall, often staging in large numbers near the Great Salt Lake. Although a few winter in California, 95 percent of all cinnamon teal winter in Mexico and Central America. They begin to return to the marshes of the intermountain region in April and March, completing their northward migration in mid-May.

BREEDING BIOLOGY

Most yearling cinnamon teal breed, and pair selection begins in late winter after the male has attained nuptial plumage. Most are paired before they reach the breeding grounds.

Home ranges are small, and the nest site is usually within 100 yards of water. As do most other duck species, cinnamon teal hens choose nest sites based more on the surrounding cover's density and the amount of overhead cover than on the actual species of plant. Some preferred plants are salt grass, and hardstem and Olney's bulrush. Most drakes stay with the hen until the third week of incubation. Clutch size averages just under nine eggs, and incubation lasts some 21 to 25 days.

Cinnamon teal hens are considered to be very attentive mothers. They brood their ducklings on small wetlands and ponds. By seven weeks, the young can fly, and the eyes of the males are turning from brown to red.

GREEN-WINGED TEAL PAIR: ©GARY KRAMER

GREEN-WINGED TEAL

Anas crecca carolinensis
Common Names: Greenwing, common teal
Average length—15 inches
Average weight—14 ounces

The smallest of our ducks, the green-winged teal is also one of the hardiest, preferring to stay in the North until the last water freezes. It is also the third-most common breeding dabbling duck in the subarctic, behind the pintail and wigeon. More than any other duck, it seeks food on mudflats when available.

Drakes in nuptial plumage have a distinctive chestnut red head with a large iridescent green patch that extends from each eye and joins at the back of the neck. Eclipse drakes resemble the female, which in turn resembles all the other mottled brown dabbler hens. Nuptial plumage starts to show in September, and is generally complete by December. Green-winged teal have a black bill, and the hen's is grayish with black specks. Their legs are gray. As you might guess from their name, the speculum is metallic green in both sexes, giving way to black toward the wing tip.

When darting in flight like a shorebird, the green-winged teal's bright white belly is usually visible, differentiating it from the mottled-brown-bellied blue-winged teal. With a wing beat almost as fast as that of diving ducks, the green-winged teal is a swift flier that often travels in much larger flocks than the other teal—frequently with as many as 50 to 100 per group.

RANGE AND MIGRATION

Few North American ducks have a breeding range as large as the green-winged teal, though in many areas it nests at low densities. The green-winged teal nests from the Aleutian Islands east through Alaska, the MacKenzie River delta, and the northern portions of all Canadian provinces. It also breeds south to central California; east through the intermountain region and central states such as Nebraska; the Great Lakes states of Minnesota and Wisconsin; and eastward yet to the Maritime Provinces. But like most dabbling ducks, the greatest density of breeding green-winged teal occurs in the Prairie Pothole Region and in the prairie parklands.

With such a large breeding range, the green-winged teal's migration patterns are complex. Alaskan birds generally migrate down the Pacific Coast and winter both in California and the west coast of Mexico. Green-winged teal nesting east of Alaska migrate south through the Central Flyway to spend winters in Texas and central Mexico, or through the northern Central Flyway states of North and South Dakota to eventually end up in Louisiana at the southern end of the Mississippi Flyway, where more than 50 percent of the continental population winters. Some continue on across the Gulf of Mexico to the Yucatan peninsula. Though there are fewer green-winged teal in the Atlantic Flyway than in all others, it is the flyway used by the most easterly breeding populations, and these birds end up in the Carolinas and Florida.

Green-winged teal migrate slowly in both spring and fall. In the autumn, they often tarry in the North until freeze-up, and most do not arrive in the wintering grounds until late November. In the spring they arrive in their more southerly breeding areas in mid-April or early May. The most northerly nesting areas may not see the arrival of green-winged teal until almost the third week of May.

BREEDING BIOLOGY

Generally breeding as yearlings, green-winged teal select mates both on the wintering grounds and during northward migration, so most hens are paired by the time they reach their nesting areas. Because of the size of their breeding range, and because green-winged teal are so small and hard to find on the nesting grounds, less is known about the formation of pair bonds or the strength of their homing instinct than about most other dabblers.

Green-winged teal are upland nesters, and seem to prefer very dense cover as nest sites. The hen lays a clutch of about eight eggs, which she incubates for about 21 days. Drakes depart as soon as incubation begins. Green-winged teal ducklings grow quickly, and can fly at 34 days.

NORTHERN SHOVELER PAIR. ©RUSSKERR.COM

NORTHERN SHOVELER

Anas clypeata
Common Names: Spoonbill, spoony,
neighbor's mallard, smiling mallard
Average length—19.5 inches
Average weight—1.5 pounds

Of the four species of shovelers found worldwide, the northern shoveler is the most colorful, has the broadest "shovel," and has the largest breeding range, which spans the north temperate portions of North America, Asia, and Europe. A medium-sized duck, the shoveler is a swift flier that often twists and turns like a teal. Because one-third of their diet is animal matter, shovelers are not considered particularly good table fare, and so are sometimes called "neighbor's mallard" (as in, I think I'll give it to my neighbor to eat).

Their other more common colloquial name is spoonbill—a descriptive name referring to the shoveler's large, spatulate bill. This bill is almost 1.5 inches wide at the tip, and though sometimes described as grotesque, it is actually a highly refined adaptation that allows shovelers to strain tiny food items from the water, utilizing foods that other ducks cannot access. When feeding in deep water with little aquatic or invertebrate life, spoonbills often cooperate in groups, spinning and stirring the water. Shovelers inhale water through the tip of their bill and eject it from the base, using the lamellae of their bill to sift plankton. In shallower water they dip their head beneath the surface, sweeping their bill from side to side as they swim slowly forward, capturing foods just above the bottom.

One of the last ducks to obtain nuptial plumage, the shoveler male doesn't don his gaudy colors until winter, whereas most dabblers at least begin to obtain their mating colors in fall. When in his nuptial plumage, the drake has a brilliant green head, a white breast, and chestnut sides. Both sexes have a pale blue patch on the forewing, similar to that of the blue-winged teal, though the drake's is brighter and larger than that of the shoveler hen. The speculum is large and iridescent green; the male's is brighter than the female's. The drake's bill is black, while the hen's is olive green to yellow with black spots. Both have orange legs.

Drakes call *who-who* and *took-took*, while the hens have a feeble, mallard-like quack.

RANGE AND MIGRATION

In North America, the northern shoveler is found in the largest numbers in the Prairie Pothole Region, followed by the parkland areas and short-grass prairies.

Although their breeding numbers decline north of the parklands, they nest as far north as Alaska and the subarctic. A few small populations breed in Canada's Maritimes, and in the wetlands of Ontario and Quebec and in Lake Erie marshes, but by far the majority nest west of the Great Lakes and north of Nebraska. Some significant populations are also found in the intermountain regions of the West.

Shovelers are early migrants and tend to leave the northern prairies by mid-October. Their population splits into two segments: One heads for California and the west coast of Mexico to winter, while the other departs for the coastal marshes of Louisiana. A much smaller number uses the Central Flyway, and most of these end up in Texas, while even fewer appear in the Atlantic Flyway, where they surface in the Carolinas. In addition, some shovelers cross the Gulf of Mexico to winter in Central America.

BREEDING BIOLOGY

As with other ducks that attain nuptial plumage quite late, shovelers do not pair until late winter. Their courtship flight is among the most energetic of ducks, and as many as 18 males will pursue a single hen. Drake shovelers are also among the most territorial of ducks, and will drive off intruders of either sex. They also tend to stay with the hen longer than drakes of other species, occasionally even until the eggs hatch.

Shovelers prefer to nest in grass, where the hen will lay about nine eggs, on average. Incubation lasts about 23 days. Northern-born shoveler ducklings can fly at about 45 days of age, while those on the southern edge of the breeding range may not fledge until they are more than 50 days old.

WOOD DUCK PAIR: ©BILLMARCHEL.COM

WOOD DUCK

Aix sponsa

Common Names: Woodie, squealer,
summer duck, acorn duck, swamp duck
Average length—18.5 inches
Average weight—1.5 pounds

The wood duck is the only North American member of the group of ducks called perching ducks, formerly the tribe Cairinini, which taxonomists recently dissolved. Most species of this former group are now considered members of tribe Anatini, the dabbling ducks.

To be sure, the wood duck shares characteristics with other dabblers. The sexes are dimorphic. Hens renest if clutches are lost. They feed in shallow waters, and they are residents of primarily freshwater habitats. But woodies differ from most of our dabblers in some important ways. Some never migrate. Some raise two broods per year. They will nest in dense communities. They habituate trees, roosting in large groups. They nest in tree cavities, not on the ground. And males only defend a mobile territory around the hen—wherever she is, the territory is—and the territory is only a few feet in diameter.

The wood duck drake is not only one of the most beautiful ducks in the world, but also one of the most beautiful of all birds. In his nuptial plumage—which he frequently attains in September, much earlier than other dabblers—he is stunning, with a green, blue, and purple tufted crown that hangs back to his neck. He can raise and fan this crown, and does so while displaying to females. He also has a distinctive white stripe that runs the length of his head from the base of the bill, up over the eyes, and through his crest. The underside of the crest is layered in white, and a white neck ring has a spur that reaches up to just beneath his eyes. The eyes themselves are bright red, rimmed in orange, and the bill, though tipped in black, is orange and white with a yellow margin at the face. To top this all off, the drake wood duck has a lovely chestnut breast, spattered with light dots, tapering to a bright white belly, and gorgeous vermiculated lemon-colored flank feathers. Finally, the tops of his wings are glazed with metallic blue, a feature also found on the hen, though hers are less intensely colored.

Still, the female wood duck is more distinctive than most dabbler hens. Rather than the mottled brown sported by so many, the wood duck hen has a white throat, chin, and belly, and her lower chest and sides are gray and brown with flecks of white. Her most distinctive feature is a tear-drop-shaped white patch that is centered on her eyes, extending back to the base of her head. Her bill is dark blue gray, and the legs and feet of both sexes are dull straw yellow.

Wood ducks' wings are proportionately wider than those of other ducks, and they have a broad, square tail. Both features seem designed to help them navigate through trees, a maneuver they perform with great skill. Though they are not the fastest of ducks on the wing, their twisting flight implies quickness. In flight they bob their head, a trait unique to them. Like other dabblers, they can spring directly into the air, and do so when startled, the hen emitting her loud *wheeek wheeeek* call, which has earned this duck the colloquial name "squealer."

Wood ducks spend a good deal of time perched in trees, though like other dabblers they feed primarily on the water.

WOOD DUCK:©SCOTT NIELSEN, DU

Wood ducks often roost in trees. They feed on the ground on acorns and other mast, as well as in shallow water in typical dabbler fashion. Some consider the wood duck as the fastest-running duck of all, and it can achieve speeds of seven miles per hour. For comparison's sake, the pheasant—long considered a champion sprinter—can run at 10 miles per hour.

RANGE AND MIGRATION

Wood ducks are confined largely to the eastern half of the U.S., south of the Great Lakes, though they are found as far north as southeastern Manitoba and southern Ontario and Quebec, and as far west as California. Very few nest in the Prairie Pothole Region, and even then are mostly confined to river bottoms where suitable trees grow. Their highest densities occur along the rivers of the upper Midwest, the coastal rivers of the Atlantic seaboard, and the Mississippi River and its tributaries in the southern part of the Mississippi Flyway. A separate but smaller population breeds in the Pacific Flyway in Idaho, Washington, Oregon, California, and British Columbia.

Since wood ducks winter in the southern half of their breeding range, migration routes are short and direct, and staging and migration areas are less distinct than those for other ducks. The state with the most wintering wood ducks is Louisiana, with nearly 500,000 birds. Other major winter concentrations occur in North and South Carolina, Georgia, and northern Florida, as well as in Mississippi, Alabama, eastern Texas, Arkansas, and western Tennessee. More than 90 per-

WOOD DUCK PAIR: ©JOE MAC HUDSPETH, JR.

Hollowed-out tree cavities make ideal nest sites for wood ducks, which take advantage of the relative safety they provide from predators.

cent of the Pacific Flyway population spends the winter in the Central Valley of California.

BREEDING BIOLOGY

Wood ducks make extensive use of bottomland hardwood forests, cypress/tupelo swamps, and forested riparian areas for breeding. They nest in natural tree cavities—frequently created by woodpeckers—as well as in artificial nest boxes. Old, mature American elm; red maple; or sweet gum trees that have been wind damaged or contain heart rot are preferred tree species. Although a few nests will be within a few feet of the ground, most often wood ducks will choose cavities 30 feet or more above the forest floor. The best cavities have an entrance large enough for the hen to enter, but too small for predators to creep in. Females, accompanied by their drake, will prospect for a suitable site, and generally select one within 50 to 150 yards of the water.

Wood duck hens are amazingly philopatric—that is, they home back to their natal site, or previous nesting area, with great precision. The drake does not home, however, and instead accompanies his mate to her home. Pair bonding begins in October and continues into winter. Drakes remain with their mates longer than most ducks, often until the eggs begin to hatch. Wood ducks nest very early, but the dates vary by latitude. Resident birds in the South begin nesting in February, while those wood ducks in northern states initiate nests in mid- to late April. In the southern populations, a few

hens raise two broods in one year, abandoning their first brood when the young can care for themselves (at six or seven weeks of age) to lay a second clutch. Wood ducks are notorious "dump" nesters—several hens may lay eggs in one nest so that a single hen will attempt to incubate as many as 40 eggs.

A normal clutch has about 12 eggs, which the hen will incubate for approximately 30 days. She lays one egg per day, usually during the morning. Once she begins incubating, she leaves the nest once in the morning, and again in the evening, to feed. When she leaves, like most other ducks, she will cover her eggs with down.

Once the ducklings have hatched, they must take a remarkable first step that other dabblers do not. Usually within 24 hours after the last duckling emerges from the egg, the hen leaves the nest, checks the area for predators, then lands on a limb, on the ground, or on water and calls to her young. Since cavities are often quite deep, the ducklings must first scramble or jump to the entrance from where, after a second's hesitation, they launch themselves into the air. Of course, they are unable to fly at this stage, so they plummet to the ground below, bouncing like rubber balls. They survive because they are so light that their rate of descent is slow and they are well cushioned by their thick layer of down. The hen then leads them to water. While wood ducks have relatively high nest success compared to ground-nesting dabblers, annual survival rates are low.

DIVING DUCKS

Tribe Aythyini

Diving ducks, also known as pochards, share many behavioral and anatomical similarities. Most are ducks of the north temperate regions, but five species occur in the Southern Hemisphere.

All divers are rather stout birds with heavy bodies and short wings, which results in a heavy wing load that requires running on the water's surface before gaining flight. They have large heads and their legs are set farther back on the body than those of dabblers. Combined with proportionately large feet, the leg position allows them to be superior divers. While diving, they do not use their wings. They do, however, use their paddle-like feet in flight as rudders.

Pochards are sexually dimorphic, although diver males are generally not as colorful as dabbler drakes, and wing plumage lacks an iridescent speculum. Instead, most diver wings are marked with a patch of white or gray. Metallic-colored plumage, where found, is usually relegated to the head.

Divers are less vocal than dabblers, and most vocalization occurs during courtship displays, which are well developed and similar among species. Much more so than dabblers, divers have a sex ratio that is highly unequal, so that males frequently far outnumber hens. Divers are monogamous, but only for one mating season, with the drakes abandoning their hen during incubation and retreating to molt. Pochard eggs are larger than those of dabblers, and nest parasitism frequently occurs in some species. Most nesting occurs over water in emergent vegetation, although redheads and lesser scaup also choose upland sites.

Usually associated with freshwater environments during the breeding season, most diver species concentrate in the winter in large numbers in coastal bays and lagoons.

In North America, we are blessed with the canvasback, redhead, ring-necked duck, and both greater and lesser scaup. Of these, only the greater scaup is found in both the Old and the New World.

CANVASBACK PAIR: ©BILL VINJE

CANVASBACK

Aythya valisineria
Common Name: Can
Average length—22 inches
Average weight—3 pounds

The aristocrat of diving ducks, the distinctive and handsome canvasback is also the least numerous of all North American diving ducks.

About the same size as mallards, canvasback are chunkier and swifter in flight, and in fact may be one of the swiftest of all waterfowl, having been clocked reliably at 74 miles per hour. Their wingbeat is rapid and noisy, and their flight is direct, with little weaving or up-and-down movement of flocks. In migration, they often fly in precise V formations.

This beautiful bird's most distinctive feature is its head, which is decidedly wedged shaped, with only a shallow dip-ping arc from the tip of their bill to the top of their fine, round head. Only some eiders share a similar profile. The bill of both males and females is black, though the hen's is sometimes dark gray. Feet are gray blue. The drake's eyes are a piercing, bright red; the hen's black.

In nuptial plumage, the male's chestnut head is rimmed beneath with a broad black band that extends around the neck and chest. His rump is also black, but his back, breast, sides, and flanks are white, and even in flight no duck shows more white than the canvasback drake. Even his nuptial-plumed wings are unique: Almost all of the wing feathers except the primaries are white. The name canvasback comes from the delicate dark vermiculations on the feathers of the back, yielding a fine wavelike pattern reminiscent of the weave of canvas. In eclipse plumage, males tend to have cinnamon brown heads and chests with gray backs, sides, and flanks. Most attain nuptial plumage by late October.

Hens have unmottled, fawn brown heads and chests, and darkly mottled brown backs and flanks. The neck frequently is so light in color, it almost appears white. The female also has a blackish rump, though not as distinct as the male.

Canvasback can dive to 30 feet, but feed most regularly in water three to 12 feet deep, where they use their wedge-like bill to dig up aquatic tubers and rootstocks. Long associated with wild celery, this bird's scientific species-specific name *valisineria* is in fact Latin for wild celery.

RANGE AND MIGRATION

Most canvasback breed in the Prairie Pothole and parkland regions, but significant numbers fly on to marshes in the subarctic, especially the Saskatchewan and Athabasca river deltas, Old Crow Flats, and interior Alaska. In the mixed grass prairie of Canada and the Dakotas, canvasback are about half as numerous as redheads, and breed at lower densities than they do in the parklands. The Minnedosa, Manitoba, area—a 4,000-square-mile area of potholes—historically has contained the greatest density of nesting canvasback, where they have exceeded 10 pairs per square mile. Canvasback are less prone

than redheads to breed in the intermountain west, but about 10,000 do use these marshes. Cans breed as far south as the Nebraska Sandhills, and east to western Minnesota.

Breeding canvasback from Alaska, British Columbia, and Alberta migrate south to winter in the Pacific Flyway. Cans from the midcontinent migrate through the three flyways to the east, using three major migration routes. The first leads from the southern Prairie Pothole Region, where they begin gathering in September, east to the upper Mississippi River near La Croix, Wisconsin, where they arrive mid-October. From there, this group of birds migrates across Wisconsin and Michigan, eventually ending up in the Mid-Atlantic states. The second major route finds canvasback continuing down the Mississippi, stopping at Pool 19, then moving on to Catahoula Lake, Louisiana. The third route begins in the northern Central Flyway, but the cans veer west to the marshes of the Great Salt Lake before crossing Nevada and ending up in the San Francisco Bay marshes. Smaller numbers of Central Flyway canvasback end up in the coastal marshes of southern Texas and the central highlands of Mexico.

Historically, the majority of canvasback wintered in the Atlantic Flyway, with the continent's largest wintering population gathering on Chesapeake Bay. However, continued pollution and other degradation of the bay, and thus its plant foods, caused a shift in canvasback migration. Of those canvasback still using the Atlantic Flyway, more now winter in the Palmico Sound area of North Carolina. Others have abandoned that flyway altogether, and now use the Mississippi and Central flyways. From 1960 to 1971, about half of all canvasback used the Atlantic Flyway, with another 25 percent in the Pacific, and 25 percent split between the two central flyways. However, beginning in the late 1980s, a pronounced shift occurred, and about 44 percent of all wintering canvasback counted on surveys were in the Mississippi and Central flyways. In fact, the largest winter concentration no longer occurs in Chesapeake Bay, but on Lake Catahoula in northern Louisiana, where up to 78,000 canvasback have been counted.

Canvasback are hardy birds, and don't flee the northern prairies until winter threatens in mid-October to early November. Most have arrived on wintering areas by December, although some begin to show in late October. They begin to depart in the spring in early February, but most retreat in late March or early April, often leaving en masse. They do not linger at migration stops during their flight north, but continue their journey so that they arrive on the prairies in mid-April. Those that must trek to the subarctic arrive there during the first and second weeks of May.

BREEDING BIOLOGY

Canvasback hens have a strong homing instinct largely independent of spring water conditions. Pairing begins in late winter, but much of it is done on the way north or even on the breeding grounds. The sex ratio of the canvasback population is heavily skewed toward males, thus there are many drakes that do not get a chance to reproduce each year. Consequently, courtship is intense and competition fierce. Long bouts of courtship displays are the norm, and exhilarating aerial pursuits are common. Nesting canvasback pairs choose an area with a complex of small to large wetlands, which they will share with other canvasback and other species. Thus actual territories are small, and seem to be mobile in nature. The male defends a small area around his mate, rather than a specific piece of geography. As she moves, so does the territory.

While they use the larger wetlands for feeding or resting, cans tend to nest on smaller marshes, often encircled by cattails or rushes, in which the hen will build her nest on a floating mat among dense plants in water from six inches to two feet deep. In some areas, sedges, phragmites cane, or flooded willows serve as nest sites. Most nest initiation occurs in late April or early May, even in the subarctic. After the hens have nested or renested, drakes depart to join other males on large marshes where they undergo their wing molt.

Canvasback eggs are large, greenish, and smooth, and the average clutch size appears to be about nine. Since canvasback nests are frequently parasitized by redheads, which will dump eggs in the canvasback nest, the tally of "true" eggs is sometimes difficult to determine. This parasitization may have a serious impact on canvasback reproduction because during the dumping, the hen redhead may roll canvasback eggs from the nest. Because redheads outnumber canvasback, the frequency of parasitic egg laying and its impact on can-

PARTIAL ALBINO CANVASBACK. ©JACK DERMID

vasback hatching success can be quite high. In fact, in some areas, more than 60 percent of canvasback nests are parasitized by redheads. The canvasback hen herself is not above parasitic egg laying, but she confines this behavior almost exclusively to laying eggs in the nest of other canvasback.

Canvasback eggs take about 24 days to hatch, after which the broods are highly mobile, seldom spending more than seven days on one marsh. Large wetlands seem to be preferred. The mother stays with the ducklings until they are almost ready to fly. Flight occurs at about 60 days of age.

Never numerous, canvasback populations have been in low numbers during most of the last half of the twentieth century. They seem particularly prone to the double assault of drought combined with increased wetland drainage on the prairies. They also have suffered from the northward movement of raccoons, a predator that easily hunts the floating vegetative mats that, for ages, protected canvasback hens. Raccoons were never recorded in most of the Prairie Pothole Region until the 1950s, and since then have prospered, thanks to the changes to the landscape wrought by man. Today raccoons present a serious predation problem for other duck species as well.

In addition, many historic canvasback migration and winter areas have been adversely affected by pollution, perhaps limiting the food sources canvasback can use, and possibly affecting winter survival and reproduction.

REDHEAD PAIR: ©BILL VINJE

REDHEAD

Aythya americana
Common Name: Redhead
Average length—20 inches
Average weight—2.5 pounds

A swift flier that always appears to be in a hurry, the redhead is a large diving duck only slightly smaller than a mallard. When coming to water, redheads sometimes drop from great heights at great speeds, creating a loud ripping roar as the air escapes their wings.

While they share a reddish head with the canvasback, the redhead is slightly smaller, is shorter necked, lacks the pronounced wedge-head shape of the can, and overall is a dark-er duck than the canvasback. The nuptial plumage of drakes, attained beginning in October, lacks the bright white back and wings of the canvasback. Instead, drake redheads are gray on the back, and darker than either canvasback or scaup. The drake's head is rounder than the canvasback's, the red head coloring is brighter, and his eyes are bright yellow or orange. Bills of both sexes are bluish gray and tipped in black, with a white ring behind the black tip. Legs and feet are gray, and the eclipse drake and hen have bottled brown backs and sides, with a white belly. Like other divers, redheads lack a colorful speculum. Instead, this area of the wing is light gray, while the covert feathers are dusky.

Redhead hens are particularly difficult to distinguish from hens of other divers. Both the ring-necked duck and the redhead have a white ring on the bill, but the redhead's head is rounder than that of the ring-necked duck, which has a small bulge at the rear. Scaup hens lack the white ring on the bill and have a white facial patch to the rear of the bill, which the redhead hen lacks.

Flocks are tight and wedged-shaped, and are usually small—five to 15 birds—except in winter, when they can gather in rafts of thousands. In migration, they frequently fly in V formation.

In spring, the drake redhead is one of the noisiest of divers, and has a loud meow call reminiscent of a cat.

RANGE AND MIGRATION

Redheads breed in both the intermountain west and the Prairie Pothole/parkland region. Some 200,000 redheads may be found annually in the intermountain's Great Basin region, with exceptionally high densities of nesting redheads in the marshes near the Great Salt Lake. North of the Prairie Pothole Region, redheads are found in significant numbers only on the deltas of the Athabasca and Saskatchewan rivers. Very few breed in Alaska, but some nest in Kansas, the Nebraska Sandhills, Minnesota, and Wisconsin, and a few as far east as Lake Erie and New York.

More than a third of all redheads migrate from Manitoba and Saskatchewan south to the gulf coast of Texas and Mexico, while another corridor from Utah leads redheads to the West Coast. A third major route takes redheads from the prairies to the Mid-Atlantic states via the Great Lakes states. About 80 percent of wintering redheads are found along the gulf coast from Apalachee Bay, Florida, west to the tip of the Yucatan peninsula. The largest concentration—as many as 300,000 redheads—occurs in Laguna Madre, Texas. In winter, redheads feed on rhizomes of shoalgrass and widgeon grass. Wintering redheads make daily flights to inland freshwater ponds to drink, since they need to dilute salt loads obtained from feeding on estuarine foods. Unlike canvasback and scaup, wintering redheads often feed primarily by submerging their heads or tipping up, instead of diving.

Redheads are the only diving duck that nests in proportionately large numbers in the U.S., so that by the time autumn rolls around, many of the birds are already at a latitude that would be southerly for other ducks. Populations continue to build as more northerly birds arrive in the intermountain and prairie regions, reaching peak numbers by mid-October. Although some redheads are already appearing at wintering areas by then, the bulk arrive in late November. In spring, redheads head north, arriving in the most southerly parts of their breeding range in March; on the north end of their range, arrival peaks in mid-May.

BREEDING BIOLOGY

Pairing begins during the winter, and continues well into April. Homing instincts for hens are not as strong as they are for canvasback. Redhead pairs tend to choose medium-sized marshes, where they usually nest over water in dense stands of vegetation, constructing bases made of matted plants attached to surrounding upright stems. Bulrush is preferred, though cattail is also used, and hens may pull standing vegetation down over them to provide more security. Nesting can occur on dry land as well.

Redheads are among the most parasitic egg-layers of all ducks. Many hens apparently lay one clutch either in the nest of other redheads, canvasbacks, or another species; then they may lay and incubate a second clutch in a nest of their own. Some appear to be strictly parasitic—that is, they lay their eggs in the nests of others, but then do not incubate a clutch of their own. Canvasback are the host of choice, since their nest requirements are similar to those of redheads. Because of this tendency to parasitize, the average size of a normal clutch is hard to determine. Incubation lasts about 24 days. Drakes abandon their hen as incubation begins.

Hen redheads are not known for their attentiveness, and frequently abandon their ducklings at an early age to fend for themselves. Broods sometimes join up, forming large groups called crèches. Most ducklings appear to be able to fly at about 60 days of age. Broods are fairly mobile, and prefer open-water areas of shallow marshes.

In the last 40 years, increased turbidity and decreased salinity caused by canal dredging in the Laguna Madre area of Texas have caused a 60 percent reduction in shoalgrass in this most important of redhead wintering areas. Biologists fear that this problem will seriously reduce the amount of food available to redheads prior to the spring migration. If so, it could in turn impact survival and perhaps reproduction, since during the winter the birds store nutrients needed for nesting.

REDHEADS: ©KIRKPATRICKWILDLIFE.COM

Redheads sometimes approach water at great speeds and from great heights, creating a ripping roar as the air escapes their wings.

GREATER SCAUP PAIR: ©ARTHUR MORRIS / BIRDS AS ART

GREATER SCAUP

Aythya marila
Common Names: Bluebill, broadbill, 'bills
Average length—18.5 inches
Average weight—2 pounds

The only pochard present both in the Old World and the New, the greater scaup is well adapted to marine environments and is the most northerly of all divers. In the Old World they breed from Norway east to Siberia, and in North America they breed primarily from Alaska to Hudson Bay.

Easily confused with the lesser scaup (found only in North America), the greater scaup is larger, weighing up to one-fifth more, and has a broader bill. The greater scaup also has a rounder, larger head than the lesser scaup, and in the drake the head color tends toward green tinged, while the lesser scaup's head color tends toward purple black. Both subspecies have yellow eyes visible from some distance. From both above and below, the nearly white trailing edge of the greater scaup's wings extends nearly to the tip, while on the lesser scaup this white area is restricted to the half nearest the body.

As you might guess, scaup, also know as bluebills, have a blue bill, and the nail at the tip is black. Females have a white crest on the cheek at the base of the bill. The bills lack the white ring found on redheads and ring-necked ducks. The

While greater scaup hens are silent, the drakes can be quite vociferous, emitting what sounds like scaup scaup, from which the species derives its common name.

GREATER SCAUP DRAKE: ©ARTHUR MORRIS / BIRDS AS ART

sides and flanks of male greater scaup are whiter than those of the lesser; the back is white gray, with vermiculation. On the water, both scaup appear much whiter in the middle and back than do drake redheads. The chest and rump of both bluebills are black, and legs and feet are gray.

Greater scaup, which feed on both vegetation and animal matter, avidly consume clams, scallops, mussels, and other bottom-dwelling shellfish, especially in winter. At times during winter, greater scaup may gather in rafts of up to 50,000 birds.

Flocks fly in compact groups, moving swiftly and erratically. Takeoffs don't come easily—scaup must run along the surface of the water for some distance before achieving flight, unless there is a stiff head wind. Hens are silent, but greater scaup drakes emit a grizzled *scaup scaup* as well as a soft dove-like crooning during courtship.

RANGE AND MIGRATION

Greater scaup breed from Hudson Bay west across the Arctic and subarctic to Alaska, where about 75 percent of all

North American greater scaup nest. A few greater scaup are also found along the east shore of James Bay to the Labrador coast and the shores of Newfoundland. Where they breed in the open boreal forest of northern Canada, they limit themselves to windswept islands on large lakes that offer tundra-like habitats similar to those they choose in the subarctic.

Even though the majority of greater scaup breed in Alaska and northwestern Canada, the primary wintering areas are in the Atlantic Flyway, requiring a long eastward trek. Since much of this migration takes place north of most human habitation, little is known about the timing or the particular migration stops. However, a significant number of these birds end up using the Great Lakes—particularly the Lake Huron and Lake Erie regions—as a part of their route before eventually depositing themselves on salt water. About 60 percent of the continent's greater scaup winter in the Atlantic Flyway from Maine to Florida, in brackish lagoons and estuaries, with the majority staying north of Chesapeake Bay.

Other populations divert from this west-east migration to drop south through Minnesota and Wisconsin to the Gulf Coast marshes of Louisiana and Texas, while some of the Alaskan greater scaup eschew the easterly route, preferring to come down the Pacific Coast or through British Columbia to winter offshore of California. A small number also winter on the Great Lakes. In recent years, the flourishing of an exotic species—the zebra mussel, brought to the Great Lakes in the bilgewater of oceangoing ships—has attracted both lesser and greater scaup to these lakes in increasing numbers. They now stop during migration to feed on zebra mussels for extended periods, especially near Point Pelee in Lake Erie. Counts of greater scaup were 75 times greater in the early 1990s than prior to the invasion of zebra mussels.

Greater scaup have been known to migrate in huge flocks. One flight of 75,000 birds reportedly arrived on Long Island, New York, on October 24, 1929.

BREEDING BIOLOGY

Pair bonds occur in late winter and early spring, and may even continue until the birds reach the breeding grounds. Greater scaup usually don't breed until their second year. Greater scaup are late nesters, with the peak of nest initiation occurring as late as mid-June in Alaska.

Greater scaup breed as isolated pairs or in small groups in most areas, although they nest in higher densities where favorable islands occur. Most nests are located in low, marshy tundra very near to the water and frequently in tall, thick grass or forbs. Nests are bowl-shaped depressions lined with mats of grass, and the hen adds considerable down to the nest once she is incubating. Clutches contain about nine eggs, which the hen cares for by herself for the 23 to 28 days it takes for them to hatch.

LESSER SCAUP PAIR: ©CLIFF BEITTEL

LESSER SCAUP

Aythya affinis
Common Names: Bluebill, 'bills
Average length—17 inches
Average weight—1.8 pounds

Considerably more numerous in North America than the greater scaup, and with a much larger breeding range, lesser scaup are the most numerous of our diving ducks.

Smaller and grayer than the greater scaup, the drake lesser scaup in breeding plumage looks black fore and aft, with white sides and a gray back. Late in the winter, and in bright light, his back can look almost white. Though black from a distance, once in hand the head shows a slightly iridescent purple, and like the greater scaup's, it has bright yellow eyes. The head of the lesser scaup is less perfectly round than that of the greater scaup, with a slight bump to the rear. The lesser scaup's bill is narrower than the greater scaup's, though it, too, is blue with a black nail at the tip. Except for an occasional very faint white ring seen on some hens, the white ring so visible on ring-necked and redhead bills is absent. The hen lesser scaup is a dark brown, mottled on the sides, but with a clear brown head. Especially in winter and spring, she has a white crescent on her cheeks between the base of the bill and her yellow eyes. Lesser scaup do not have a colorful speculum;

instead, their secondaries are white gray, tipped with brown. In the greater scaup, this white band extends nearly to the tips of the wings.

Lesser scaup hens are not very vocal compared to dabbler hens, but are more vociferous than greater scaup hens. In flight they frequently call with a guttural *brrtt brrtt*, while the drake has a discordant *scaup scaup*.

Lesser scaup are much more likely to visit small lakes than are greater scaup, and they are swift fliers with very rapid wing beats and often travel in compact flocks of 25 to 50 birds. In winter, much of their food is animal matter—clams, crayfish, and aquatic insects. Where available, however, they will also eat large amounts of aquatic grasses, seeds, wild celery, and wild rice. Although they use salt water and brackish marshes, they are less restrictive than greater scaup.

RANGE AND MIGRATION

Except for a few small breeding colonies east of James Bay and around the Great Lakes, the vast majority of lesser scaup breed in a huge region that begins south of Hudson Bay, dips south through Minnesota and the Dakotas, and then sweeps northwest through Montana to the Canadian northwest and into interior Alaska before swinging back again to Hudson Bay. Minor breeding populations occur in British Columbia, Utah, northern California, Oregon, and Washington. More than 600,000 lesser scaup breed in surveyed areas of Alaska, and similar densities occur in the forested parts of the

MacKenzie River Valley and Old Crow Flats. The Slave River parklands have the highest recorded density of lesser scaup, and significant breeding occurs in the Saskatchewan and Peace-Athabasca River deltas. Although the boreal forest supports low densities of scaup, its contribution is huge because the region is so vast, and indeed about 70 percent of these ducks nest in this kind of habitat. The prairie parklands and the prairie potholes contribute fewer scaup, and represent the southern edge of significant breeding efforts.

About 60 percent of lesser scaup winter in the Mississippi Flyway, with most of these spending the winter in Louisiana's lakes, coastal marshes, and the open waters of the Gulf of Mexico. The Atlantic Flyway is the winter home to about 30 percent of lesser scaup, most of which winter in Florida. Only about 6 percent winter in the Pacific Flyway, and even fewer (3 percent) winter in the Central Flyway.

Several migration corridors extend from the boreal forest and northern prairies east to the Atlantic, either just north of, through, or just south of the Great Lakes. Attracted by the food made available from the expansion of the exotic zebra mussel introduced to the Great Lakes from bilgewater belched from oceangoing vessels, lesser scaup now gather in both spring and fall on these lakes in much larger numbers than they did historically.

Two significant migration corridors funnel scaup off the prairies, where they gather in early autumn. One dives south through Minnesota to Illinois, then on to eastern Louisiana and the gulf. A parallel skyway from the Dakotas takes lesser scaup south through the prairie states to western Louisiana and the gulf. From here, some of both populations flow across to the east coast of Mexico and the Yucatan peninsula.

Lesser scaup leave their most northerly breeding areas in September, and pass through the mid-latitude states from mid-October to mid-November. In spring, they begin to head north as the ice melts, arriving in the prairie parklands about mid-April, and in Alaska and the subarctic in mid- to late May.

BREEDING BIOLOGY

It appears that many hen lesser scaup do not breed until they are two years old. Some may wait until they are three. Since males far outnumber hens, some drakes may never breed during their lifetime. Lesser scaup begin to pair on the wintering grounds, but much of the courtship takes place during the northward migration, with most hens paired with a partner by time they reach the nesting grounds.

Late nesters, lesser scaup may not begin nesting until late May or mid-June, and, apparently, the latitude of nesting does not affect the actual calendar date. Pairs seek out territories near deeper, more permanent wetlands, and the hen prefers to nest in wet meadows near water. However, upland areas near water, as well as islands, are also used. As eggs are laid, the hen builds up the rim of the nest from bits of surrounding vegetation. Although she will add some down to the nest, lesser scaup nests contain less down than nests of most other ducks. The hen

will lay an average of nine eggs, and will incubate them for about 25 days. The drake departs early in incubation.

Occasionally while the ducklings are still in down, and frequently by the time they are four or five weeks old, the hen will abandon her brood so she can retreat to molt. Broods will often join into large groups, sometimes watched over by one or two hens. Lesser scaup usually reach flight stage sometime around their 50th day of life.

LESSER SCAUP DRAKE: ©RUSSKERR.COM

At home in large and small lakes, bays, marshes, and estuaries, lesser scaup feed primarily on animal matter such as clams, mussels, and aquatic insects.

RING-NECKED DUCK PAIR: ©SCOTT NIELSEN, DU

RING-NECKED DUCK

Aythya collaris
Common Names: Ring-billed duck,
ringbill, blackjack
Average length—17 inches
Average weight—1.6 pounds

This delightful little pochard is exclusive to North America, breeding across a broad swath of northern forest from the Maritimes to Great Slave Lake. Of all the divers, the ring-necked duck is much more likely to visit small bodies of freshwater, including beaver ponds. It rises into flight more easily than other divers, which may explain why it is comfortable even on small ponds. Ring-necked ducks fly in smaller flocks—15 to 20 birds—than do scaup, which they resemble, and they are swift, often dropping from great heights to wheel around a lake at treetop level. Largely a silent duck, they do make considerable chortling noises while feeding, which can be heard on still nights, especially when they gather in large flocks during migration.

RING-NECKED DUCKS: ©SCOTT NIELSEN, DU

Poorly named, the drake ring-necked duck's thin chestnut neck ring is barely visible, even under the best of conditions. Hunters commonly call this bird ringbill, which is a much more descriptive name. Both the hen and the drake ring-necked duck have distinct white rings around their blue bills, immediately to the rear of the black bill tip. Only the redhead has a similar ring near the tip. In addition, the male ring-necked duck's bill is outlined with white where it joins his face. The head of the ring-necked duck is decidedly square near the rear, which helps distinguish it from scaup and redheads, even in hens. While the gray backs of both scaup drakes appear nearly white in good light, the ring-necked drake's back always appears black, and both sexes tend to sit with a more upright head than do the scaup. While on the water, the drake in nuptial plumage shows a white triangle just in front of his wings that points upward toward the base of his neck. The drake's eyes are bright yellow; the hen's are dark, but usually rimmed in white. Feet and legs are gray blue.

Ring-necked ducks favor vegetable matter, and some of the largest gatherings on the continent occur during October in the wild rice lakes of Minnesota and Wisconsin, where these long-distance travelers pause to refuel on this favorite food.

RANGE AND MIGRATION

The ring-necked duck likes neither the subrctic nor the prairies for breeding, and instead nests in a broad swath across the northern and boreal forests of the U.S. and Canada; south to a line from Maine to Minnesota; then northwest through the prairie parklands to northwestern Canada just beyond Great Slave Lake; and back east again through the southern halves of the eastern Canadian provinces to the Maritimes. The species only began breeding in the eastern part of the continent in the 1930s, but now is established and seems to be pioneering. The greatest number of nesting ring-necked ducks occurs in the closed boreal forest of northern Alberta, Saskatchewan, and Manitoba. The highest densities occur on the quality wetlands of the Saskatchewan and Athabasca river deltas, and the Slave River parklands. About 25,000 ring-necked ducks breed in the Great Lakes states, and an equal number in the mountain valleys and basins from California to British Columbia.

As with the scaup, the autumn migration of ring-necked ducks has an eastward tendency. Routes extend from the prairie provinces to Ontario, then on to the eastern U.S., eventually to end in South Carolina and Florida. Northern Minnesota, Wisconsin, and the Upper Peninsula of Michigan are major staging areas during autumn, and many of these birds will also continue on east to winter in Florida and South Carolina. Others turn south here, and continue on to Louisiana and the east coast of Texas. Only a few winter west of the Great Plains. More than one-half of the Atlantic Flyway ringbills winter in Florida, concentrating in the Lake Okeechobee area. Several thousand move on to the West Indies. In the Mississippi Flyway, many are found from Tennessee to Louisiana.

Their fall passage begins in September, with numbers building on traditional northern states staging areas until mid-October, after which time numbers rapidly dwindle. The main portion reach their wintering areas in mid-November. In spring, they begin to leave the winter areas in February, with the pace increasing through March. They arrive in their nesting grounds, depending on latitude, from early April to May.

BREEDING BIOLOGY

Pair bonding begins as early as October, but continues even during the spring migration. Ring-necked ducks favor shallow marshes that have some woody vegetation around the perimeter, where they will nest in the marsh on clumps of floating plants, most commonly sedge, but nests can be up to 80 feet from water. The nest itself is nothing more than a few flattened leaves at first, but as the hen lays her fifth or sixth egg, she builds up the perimeter into a cup, and may even weave overhead plants into a canopy. Once the third to last egg is laid, she adds a considerable amount of down from her breast. Drake ring-necked ducks tend to stay with the hen longer than drake scaup stay with their mates—often into the fourth week of incubation. Nesting usually occurs in May, and clutches average nine eggs, which take about 26 days to hatch. Most hens stay with their broods until they can fly, an event that occurs seven to eight weeks after hatching.

130

SEA DUCKS

Tribe Mergini

Fourteen species of sea ducks span the world, including the tropics, but most are subarctic, Arctic, or north-temperate dwellers. As you might guess by their name, many are suited for life on or near the sea, but several exist primarily in freshwater and spend most of their life inland.

Accomplished divers, some can remain submerged for more than two minutes, and the oldsquaw has been known to dive to depths of 200 feet—the record for ducks.

Mergansers all have in common the fact that they are primarily fish eaters, though they will also feed on crustaceans, frogs, leeches, and salamanders. Their long, saw-like, tapered bill with its hooked tip is well designed for catching fish, and they are capable divers.

Scoters are chunky sea ducks that are noted for flying so low to the water that they barely clear the crests of waves. All fly in loose, stringy flocks, and the buzzing sound of their wing beats can be heard up to a half mile away on calm days. While traversing the coasts, they tend to fly around points and islands, rather than over them. Primarily carnivorous, they feed largely on mollusks and shellfish, and have powerful gizzards that can crush the hardest of shells. All scoters of both sexes are essentially black in color, though hens do display some brown mottling on the belly and sides.

The highly specialized eiders of the Arctic and subarctic are almost completely marine in their nonbreeding habitats.

Thick necked and stocky, eiders are superb divers that feed most of the year on mussels, clams, barnacles, and other animal foods. Strong jaws and a wide, wedge-shaped bill allow them to pry mussels from rocks, which they bring to the surface to crush and eat. A powerful gizzard grinds shells into fine pieces. Eiders also feed in shallow marine estuaries or tundra ponds, where they tip up much like dabblers, or tread the bottom with their large feet to expose various animal foods. Some feed on tidal flats during falling tides. Large, supraorbital salt glands allow them to ingest salt water and marine prey without notable adverse effects.

Weighing up to six pounds, eiders rise slowly from the water, and fly alternately flapping and sailing in flocks strung out in a line. Mass migrations of some species are not unusual—in May, 1976, some 360,000 king eiders crossed Point Barrow, Alaska, in a 10-hour period. Molt migrations are also typical, with males and nonbreeding birds flying far out to sea to molt while breeding hens incubate.

All eiders are extremely sexually dimorphic. Males tend toward black and white—with white backs and black sides—and a variety of colorful head and bill configurations. Eider females resemble dabbler hens for their exceptionally effective mottled brown camouflage, a real advantage for birds that frequently nest in plain sight on nearly bare tundra, though the brown tends to be a bit rustier than that of the dabbler.

Many eiders are very philopatric, returning to the same nest site year after year. Since most don't breed until two or three years of age, and because the clutch size is very small—only two to six eggs—eiders have low reproductive potential. In addition, most do not attempt to renest if the clutch is lost, most likely because the breeding season is so very short. Nests are typically in shallow depressions, and lined with large amounts of their famous eiderdown. The hens of most species rarely leave to feed during the 22 to 28 days of incubation, and may lose up to 40 percent of their body weight. Large amalgamations of broods are common, tended to by one or two hens, freeing many other hens to attend to their molt and to feed so that they can regain lost weight. The sex ratio in eider populations is skewed heavily in favor of males, which, as you might predict, leads to aggressive competition between drakes during courting season.

Typically, eiders winter as far north as open water exists, sometimes gathering in huge flocks. They seem unbothered by frigid air temperatures, and will even loaf on pack ice. Four species of eider breed in North America.

WHITE-WINGED SCOTER PAIR: ©WAYNE LYNCH

COMMON MERGANSER PAIR: ©SCOTT NIELSEN, DU

133

BUFFLEHEAD PAIR: ©W. STEVE SHERMAN

BUFFLEHEAD

Bucephala albeola
Common Names:
Butterball, dipper, helldivers
Average length—14.5 inches
Average weight—1 pound

Able to leap into the air more like a dabbler, the swift-flying bufflehead is the smallest of our sea ducks. Drakes weigh only a pound, and hens barely eight ounces. They eat primarily aquatic insects in the summer, snails and clams in the winter.

The male in nuptial plumage, attained in September, is distinctive for his bright white cheek patch that angles upward to the rear. His head tends toward rusty purple below the patch, and dark, metallic green blue on the face and above the patch. His tail is long, and the center of his back is dark, but he has a bright white stripe, which is visible in flight, from the front to back of the wings. The hen's white wing area is limited to the speculum, and her brown head sports a small white cheek patch behind the eyes. Both sexes have a short, blue black bill; the drake's feet are pink, the hen's are blue gray. Eyes are brown. Chests of males are white; hens and immature drakes tend to have mottled gray chests. The bellies of all are white.

Combined with the white patches on cheeks and wings, the overall impression of the butterball on the wing is of black and white.

RANGE AND MIGRATION

Bufflehead nest across the northern forests of Canada, from Quebec through the prairie parklands, northwest to the Yukon. They also are found in interior Alaska, and in lesser numbers on the Alaskan coast. They prefer standing or slow-moving waters in a forested setting, and nest in tree cavities, most of which have been excavated by the flicker. Like other tree nesters, they have a strong homing instinct. Bufflehead tend to migrate just ahead of freeze-up, moving in small flocks of five or six birds. Large gatherings are rare. They winter as far north as the Great Lakes, but most move to either the Atlantic or the Pacific coast, or to the Gulf of Mexico.

BREEDING BIOLOGY

Pair bonding doesn't occur until their northward migration, sometime in March. Males are aggressive toward each other, often fight, and perform elaborate and prolonged courtship displays. Hens lay clutches of about nine eggs, which take 29 to 31 days to hatch. After 24 hours, the ducklings jump from the tree to the ground, where they are led to water. Males play no role in incubation or brooding, and move to different areas to molt. Hens abandon broods after about six weeks to perform their own molt, and broods sometimes combine and fend for themselves, or are adopted by a single hen. They can fly at 50 days of age.

COMMON GOLDENEYE PAIR: ©SCOTT NIELSEN, DU

COMMON GOLDENEYE

Bucephala clangula americana
Common Name: Whistler
Average length—19 inches
Average weight—2.5 pounds

The rapid wing beat of the common goldeneye yields a whirring, whistling sound, and the ducks are often heard before seen. Although it is a black-and-white bird on the wing, its much larger size (over twice as heavy) than the outwardly similarly colored bufflehead helps distinguish the two species. More prone to eat vegetable matter than the bufflehead, the goldeneye nonetheless depends on snails, clams, crayfish, and similar foods in winter.

Common goldeneye drakes have a black, high-crowned, angular head, tinged with glossy green. They also have bright gold eyes—hence their name—though the hen's are much paler yellow. Drakes sport a dime-sized white spot immediately behind the base of the bill, while the hen's head is chocolate brown and lacks this spot. Both sexes have blackish primaries, and both have a white speculum, but the drake's wing coverts have additional white. A distinctive marker in flight, the white contrasts sharply with the black back, rump, and tail. The chest, sides, belly, and neck of the male are bright white; the hen shares the white neck and belly, but her sides and back are dabbled gray. Both sport yellow feet and legs, and gray bills. The hen's bill becomes tipped with yellow come spring.

RANGE AND MIGRATION

Goldeneyes are tree cavity nesters, and their breeding range encompasses much of the Canadian forest from coast to coast, as well as the northern states of the U.S. and Alaska. One of the last ducks to migrate in autumn, the goldeneye is a harbinger of winter to all who live in the north. One-third of the population winters along the Atlantic, from Newfoundland to Florida, concentrating from North Carolina to Long Island Sound. One-half winter on the Pacific, from the Aleutian Islands to Washington State, though some move as far south as California. The remainder are scattered throughout the Great Lakes and the Mississippi Flyway.

BREEDING BIOLOGY

Nesting peaks near the end of April, and pair bonding occurs in March. Goldeneye drakes are noted for their elaborate courtship display, in which they tilt their head so that it lies nearly on the back, bill skyward, while thrashing furiously with their legs, kicking up spurts of water. Hens usually don't breed until two years of age, and select tree cavities as high as 60 feet from the ground. They lay about nine eggs, though competition for suitable cavities often leads to dump nesting. Incubation lasts about 30 days, and 24 hours after hatching, the ducklings are called to the nest hole where they leap bravely out and flutter to earth. They will be able to fly in about 60 days, and hens frequently abandon them well before that time. Postbreeding birds often move north to molt, prior to migration.

BARROW'S GOLDENEYE PAIR: ©JACK MILLS

BARROW'S GOLDENEYE

Bucephala islandica
Common Names: Whistler,
Rocky Mountain whistler
Average length—19 inches
Average weight—2.75 pounds

The Barrow's goldeneye is the ecological equivalent in the West of the common goldeneye, and the two are so nearly identical that it is difficult to tell them apart on the wing. The white cheek patch of the Barrow's drake is crescent shaped; the common's is round. The females of the two species are essentially identical, except for the difference in head shape.

RANGE AND MIGRATION

The Barrow's goldeneye breeds primarily in the intermountain regions of the western U.S., Canada, and Alaska, as well as in the Cascade Mountains, the Sierras, and Wyoming. A small eastern population breeds in Labrador.

The western population winters in coastal marine and estuary environments from California north to Alaska's Aleutian Islands. The small eastern population winters in the Gulf of St. Lawrence, and along the Atlantic Coast.

BREEDING BIOLOGY

Essentially the same as the common goldeneye (see previous page).

HARLEQUIN DUCK PAIR: ©ADRIAN DORST

HARLEQUIN DUCK

Histrionicus histrionicus
Common Name: Harlequin
Average length—17 inches
Average weight—1.5 pounds

This small duck is named after Harlequin, the clown of eighteenth-century Italian comic opera, thanks to the drake's gaudy and theatrical plumage. Indeed, the harlequin drake is one of the most striking ducks of all.

Drakes have an elaborate pattern of black, white, indigo, and chestnut that contrasts with the glossy slate blue gray plumage of their back, wings, head, and chest. A white facial crescent is followed by a white dot behind the eyes, which themselves are followed by a white slash down either side of the mane. A circular white ring runs round the base of the neck, and another precedes the wings. The speculum is metallic blue. Hens lack all of these distinctive markings and are dark brown, with mottled gray on the breast and belly.

The harlequin breeds in Siberia, northern Asia, Iceland, and Greenland. In North America, its breeding range is very similar to that of the Barrow's goldeneye. Both in freshwater and in salt water, harlequins feed largely on animals such as crustaceans, mollusks, crabs, and insects.

Nesting occurs in June, and hens select nest sites along swift mountain streams among brush or in crevices in rocks. They lay about six eggs, which take 28 or 29 days to hatch.

OLDSQUAW PAIR: ©IRENE HINKE-SACILOTTO

OLDSQUAW

Clangula hyemalis
Common Names: Sea pintail,
long-tailed duck, cockertail
Average length—20.5 inches
Average weight—2 pounds

The most vocal of sea ducks, old-squaws' melodious, rhythmical calls and yodeling are the voice of the tundra. Circumpolar in distribution, the oldsquaw lives as far north as land exists, and is the most common duck in the Arctic. They are the deepest diving of ducks, capable of submerging to more than 200 feet.

Drakes have long pintail-like tails, which they carry at a 45-degree angle when floating. The female is primarily brown with a mottled white head in winter and grows progressively darker by spring.

Oldsquaw pair in late winter, and some may remain bonded for more than one season. They nest across North America in the Arctic and subarctic, placing nests on the ground near ponds or the sea. They lay about eight eggs, which are incubated by the hen for approximately 26 days. Ducklings develop more swiftly than do those of prairie ducks.

In North America, oldsquaw winter along both ocean coasts, from the Aleutians to northern California in the Pacific, and from Labrador to North Carolina in the Atlantic. They also winter throughout the Great Lakes and the Gulf of St. Lawrence.

RED-BREASTED MERGANSER DRAKE. ©CLIFF BEITTEL

MERGANSERS

Common

Hooded

Red-Breasted

The red-breasted merganser (*Mergus serrator*) is named for the cinnamon breasts of the drakes. Both sexes have a shaggy crest, and show white on their wing tops, though the male's is more extensive. Their flight is strong and direct, and almost always low over the water.

Nesting farther north than other mergansers, they are the only subarctic fish-eating duck. In addition to nesting in tundra environments, they also nest throughout the boreal forest, from Newfoundland west to northern British Columbia and Alaska. They are ground nesters, usually locating nests under limbs or brush, or in rock crevices. Ducklings are abandoned at an early age, and several broods usually form into large

groups attended by a single female. At 23 inches and 2.5 pounds, it is the second largest of our mergansers.

Most red-breasted mergansers winter in the Atlantic, gulf, or Pacific maritime environments, though significant numbers use the Great Lakes. In spring, they migrate north later than the other mergansers.

Larger and showing much more white, the common merganser (*Mergus merganser*) is circumpolar in distribution. Drakes may weigh as much as five pounds, though most average 2.5 pounds, and are about 25 inches long. The drake's green head lacks the crest found on other mergansers, though the female's rusty brown head may show a shaggy mane. Common mergansers breed throughout the boreal and mixed forest regions of North America—from New England and Newfoundland in the east, across the lake states and Canadian Provinces—to British Columbia and Alaska. They are cavity nesters, and are among the earliest ducks to nest. Broods of ducklings sometimes hitch rides on the backs of hens, and several broods quite commonly combine into large groups, attended by a single hen.

Most common mergansers winter in the Mississippi and Central flyways, though lesser numbers are found in the other two flyways; they winter primarily on freshwater. They are among the last ducks to migrate south.

The drake hooded merganser sports plumage that makes it the handsomest of all mergansers. This one has its crest expanded in full display to attract a mate.

The handsomest of mergansers is the little hooded merganser (*Mergus cucullatus*), and the drakes sport lovely barred tawny brown sides, a striped black-and-white chest, white-edged tertials (which the hen shares) on their wings, and a crested black head with a white band that can be erected and fanned. Females also have a crested head, but are largely brown and gray all over. Bellies are typically white in autumn and winter—the drake's is whiter than the hen's.

Both sexes have a long but blunt tail, which helps them maneuver through forests, and other than the tertials, there is little white shown on the wings. Short wing strokes imply great speed, and the ducks usually fly in groups of two or three.

Their range and highest breeding density centers in the forested region around the Great Lakes, though some breed in bottomland forests and riparian environments as far west as the Prairie Pothole Region, south and east through the central U.S., and south to Louisiana. Another population breeds from Washington State through British Columbia, into the Alaskan panhandle. As with other mergansers, they do not nest until they are two years of age, and these 18-inch, 1.5-pound birds are cavity nesters that may select sites as high as 75 feet.

Hooded mergansers winter in bottomland forest wetlands and in estuarine and freshwater coastal marshes. Nearly two-thirds winter in the Mississippi Flyway, and about one-quarter in the Atlantic. The western population winters from British Columbia to Mexico. In spring, hooded mergansers are among the first ducks to begin the northward migration.

SURF SCOTER DRAKE ©CLIFF BEITTEL

SCOTERS
Surf
White-winged
Black

The surf scoter (*Melanitta perspicillata*) is the only scoter whose breeding range is limited to North America. The drake has a bulbous, multi-colored bill that has an elaborate pattern of yellow, black, and white, and red orange colors. He also sports a white crest on his forehead, and another white patch on the back of his head. It is the only scoter to display this much white on or near the head, which, combined with the odd bill, makes identification easy. Legs and feet are crimson.

The surf scoter breeds in boreal forests from Alaska, east through the Canadian northwest to Hudson Bay, and in north-ern Quebec and Labrador. Nests are built in well-concealed ground locations, frequently under low spreading branches of conifers, and eggs are laid in late June and July.

This 19.5-inch, two-pound scoter winters on both coasts, but is more common in the Pacific than the Atlantic, and is in fact the most common scoter to winter on the West Coast. Eastern wintering populations are found from Nova Scotia to Florida, but are densest near New Jersey and Virginia. In the Pacific, they winter from the Aleutian Islands to Mexico. Surf scoters are not uncommon on the Great Lakes, and they occasionally frequent the Gulf of Mexico.

The black scoter (*Melanitta nigra*) is the least abundant North American scoter, though it is also found across northern Europe and Asia. Black scoters are among the most musical of ducks, and drakes are noted for metallic, high-pitched calls. Drakes are jet black except for yellow swelling on the base of the upper bill; hens are mottled brown with a dark gray bill. The drake is the only northern duck that has entirely black plumage.

The black scoter's North American breeding range is poorly defined, but the bird is known to breed along the Bering Sea coast of Alaska, and there are also reports of some breeding occurring near Hudson Bay, as well as in Quebec and Newfoundland. Black scoters nest beneath tall, concealing vegetation in nests constructed of grasses and lichens; the nests are filled with copious amounts of dark down.

WHITE-WINGED SCOTER DRAKE ©ARTHUR MORRIS / BIRDS AS ART

Black scoters winter from the Aleutians to southern California on the Pacific Coast, as well as from Nova Scotia to Florida on the Atlantic Coast.

Unlike the other two North American scoters, the white-winged scoter (*Melanitta fusca*) displays, as you might guess by the name, a broad white band on its secondaries. Drakes also have a comma-shaped dab of white around and beneath their eyes. At 21.5 inches and 3.5 pounds, it is the largest scoter, and, indeed, one of the largest ducks. This species is also found in northern Europe and Asia.

White-winged scoters nest farther south than any other scoter, and have been reported nesting in North Dakota. Most, however, breed from Quebec's James Bay coastal plain on the east to the subarctic coast on the north, and through central Alaska to the Bering Sea on the west. Historically, they were far more common in the prairie regions. They prefer to nest on islands in permanent lakes or in nearby woods. They do not breed until they are two years old, and many may wait until age three. Although solitary breeders most of the time, on islands they may nest in colonies. Broods often join to form large groups, and ducklings can fly at about eight weeks of age.

White-winged scoters winter on both oceanic coasts. In the Atlantic, the largest gatherings are found from Long Island Sound to Chesapeake Bay, and off the shoals of Nantucket and Cape Cod. In the Pacific, they winter from southeast Alaska to the Baja peninsula.

DRAKES AND HEN KING EIDERS. ©WAYNE LYNCH

EIDERS
Common, King,
Spectacled, Steller's

The king eider (*Somateria spectabilis*), in addition to breeding across northern Russia, Siberia, and Greenland, is found from Hudson Bay in the east to the Bering Strait in Alaska. The majority of North American king eiders breed at dispersed inland sites in the central and western Arctic, where they use both fresh and salt water for brood rearing. They are solitary nesters, unlike other eiders, which often nest in colonies. They winter in the Bering Sea, in the northern Gulf of Alaska, and near Newfoundland and Labrador.

The drake king eider is spectacularly beautiful. He has a puffy blue head to the top and rear, an ivory wedge-shaped cheek patch that has the eye at the narrow end of the wedge, and a fleshy yellow knob outlined in black that graces both sides of the face immediately behind a crimson bill. Hens tend to have a rusty tinge to their dappled brown feathers, and a sloping forehead reminiscent of the canvasback.

Biologists have little data on king eider populations because of the species' remote nesting grounds, and since these birds winter far out to sea. It is believed that more than 1 million may nest in North America, and that their population has been declining since the 1960s.

The most numerous of North American eiders is the common eider (*Somateria mollissima*), which is also the largest of northern ducks. Four subspecies are recognized in North America. All drakes have some amount of yellow on the base of their neck and back of their head, and a glossy black cap on top.

The first subspecies, the American eider (*S.m. dresseri*) breeds along the Atlantic Coast from central Labrador south to Maine, and winters as far south as Massachusetts. They are noted for the drake's forehead dome, and large round frontal "processes" (yellowish fleshy extensions of the bill that reach back along the face nearly to the eyes—all common eiders have this feature to some degree). Despite some local declines in Quebec and Nova Scotia, the American eider population seems to be growing.

Another subspecies, the Pacific eider (*S.m. v-nigra*) breeds on Victoria Island, the Northwest Territories, the West Beaufort Sea, and the Bering Sea coasts of Alaska, and winters on the Bering Sea and as far south as British Columbia. Weighing up to six pounds, they are as big as some geese, and drakes have an orange bill and tapered, narrow processes, as well as a black V on their white throat.

Northern eiders (*S.m. borealis*) breed along the coasts of Greenland, Baffin Island, and Southampton Island, and along the north and central coasts of Labrador. They spend their winters in the Gulf of St. Lawrence and in the Atlantic along the coasts of the Maritime Provinces and northern Maine. The drake's frontal processes are short and narrow, and the bill tends toward gray green.

Finally, the last of the North American common eiders is the Hudson Bay eider (*S.m. sedentaria*), found only on islands and along the coasts of Hudson and James bays, where the population stays throughout the year. The frontal processes of the drake are less extensive but similar to those of the American eider.

The spectacled eider (*Somateria fischeri*) is named for the large silvery white patches that surround the drake's eyes, yielding the look of eyeglasses or old-fashioned aviator's goggles. Black rimmed, the "goggles" are made up of fine satin feathers, and hens and even ducklings display this feature, though the rusty brown hen's eye patches are brown gray. Spectacled eiders are the only ducks that have feathers that cover the bill nearly to the nostrils, and the bill and forehead are sloped similar to that of the canvasback. The bill feathers of hens are brown, but sometimes with a saddle of pale yellow. On the drake, these feathers are white near the nostrils, followed by a broken band of black, then buffy yellow back to the ivory eye patch. Spectacled eiders are about 15 percent smaller than the common eider.

Spectacled eiders nest in a narrow swath along the coast of Alaska, as well as in Siberia. Solitary nesting is the norm, but

KING EIDER: ©MASLOWSKI PHOTO

The drake king eider is regal and resplendent with a blue head, ivory cheek patch, and, during the breeding season, a distinctive yellow nob above its crimson bill.

small colonies do form, and they frequent tidal pools and tundra ponds where they dabble like mallards. Subadults are seldom seen on the nesting grounds, so probably spend the season out to sea.

Until recently, no one knew where spectacled eiders wintered, but in 1995 researchers with the U.S. Fish and Wildlife Service homed in on the signal of a female fitted with a satellite transmitter. The ducks were found far out to sea—south of St. Lawrence Island, midway between Alaska and Siberia—feeding and loafing in holes in the vast pack ice.

The Steller's eider (*Polysticta stellari*), the smallest of our eiders, historically bred throughout coastal Alaska, as well as in Siberia, but the range has recently shrunk to a small area of the Arctic coastal plain near Barrow, Alaska, and eastern Siberia. They winter from Kodiak Island west along the south coast of Alaska to the eastern Aleutians.

Females of the species are a very uniform dark brown black, but the males have a black back with a buttery yellow breast awash with light rusty brown; a broad black neck band and underchin; and a white head with black eye patches. They lack the elaborate bill or frontal processes of other eiders, but the drake does have a dirty yellow patch of feathers between its gray green bill and its eyes, and a strange little knob of green yellow feathers at the very back of its head, often underlined in black. The bill is smaller and more dabbler-like, and has a fleshy outer edge. Stellar's eiders tend to feed on much smaller animal items, like the little blue mussel and razor clams, than do other eiders.

These eiders tend to nest in June or July in shallow depressions made of tundra mosses near the ocean, but adjacent to freshwater ponds, lakes, or calm sections of rivers.

Stiff-Tailed Ducks

Tribe Oxyurini

These mainly freshwater ducks with their conspicuous upright cocked tails are found on all continents except Antarctica. Almost entirely aquatic, stiff-tailed ducks dive as a response to danger, rather than flush, and are capable of sinking slowly, barely leaving a ripple. With the exception of one species, they lack any metallic coloration or speculum. Most are found in the Southern Hemisphere in tropical or subtropical habitats, and they are fond of small, shallow, and heavily vegetated fresh or brackish waters avoided by other diving ducks.

Two species are found in North America—the ruddy duck and the masked duck. The former is abundant here; the latter is rare.

The masked duck (*Oxyura dominica*) is found primarily in South and Central America and Mexico, but occasionally appears in the U.S. This small duck, rusty in color with black mottling, sports a black face mask on the drake, while the female is mottled brown with a buff head that has two lateral black stripes—one through the eye, and one just below it. They occasionally appear in Texas and Florida, as well as other gulf coast states. They have bred in Texas on several occasions.

RUDDY DUCK PAIR. ©RON SPOMER

RUDDY DUCK

Oxyura jamaicensis
Common Names: Bull-necked teal, dollar duck
Average length—15.5 inches
Average weight—1.3 pounds

The drake of this strange and delightful little duck, when in nuptial plumage and performing his elaborate courtship display, buzzes like some amazing bathtub toy around the surface of lakes, emitting a weird conglomeration of sounds, throwing spray, and generating bubbles. Even when not courting, the drake ruddy duck is hard to mistake, thanks to the jaunty angle at which he holds his tail.

Unlike most other ducks, the ruddy drake doesn't attain his breeding plumage until late in the winter, and holds onto it in the summer. Consequently, when they migrate in the autumn, both sexes are mottled brown on the bottom (though the hen is lighter), with gray backs and dark heads. The male has a blacker head with a white mask beneath the eyes, and the contrast between these two increases as the nuptial plumage is gained. The female has a buff-colored mask that is divided by a broken brown band. Both have gray wings; gray legs and feet; broad, short, gray bills; and long tails made of exceptionally stiff feathers.

In breeding plumage, the drake is a handsome red brown on the back, and his broad bill turns sky blue. The feathers above the eyes lengthen and grow erect, giving him a devilish look. The mask grows snow white and the top half of the head becomes glossy black.

Courtship displays are most unusual. They begin in winter but continue when the birds reach the breeding grounds. The drake assumes a cocky posture, with his tail erect so that the tail feathers actually lean over his back almost to the nape of the neck, exposing his white rump. He elevates his "horns" and pumps his bill faster and faster against his chest and the inflated air sacs on his trachea, resulting in a hollow thumping sound. While doing all this, he also forces air from his breast feathers by compacting them, resulting in a band of bubbles forming in the water. Competing males have been known to tear into each other, fighting like bantam chickens.

RANGE AND MIGRATION

Breeding takes place primarily in the Prairie Pothole and parklands regions, but a few nest as far north as Great Slave Lake, and significant breeding also takes place in western Minnesota and the intermountain marshes.

More than half of all ruddy ducks winter in the Pacific Flyway. About one-quarter head east to the Atlantic Flyway, with the remainder divided between the two middle flyways. Large gatherings occur during the migration, particularly in the Klamath Basin of northern California, where more than 100,000 ruddies have been known to pause. Other intermountain marshes attract bunches of 2,000 to 30,000 ruddy ducks.

Ruddy ducks gather in September, and the peak of migration occurs in mid-October. Most migration takes place at night. The earliest ruddies appear in wintering areas at the end of September, but most arrive in late November and into December. In spring, ruddies begin migrating north in February, with the exodus increasing into April. By the last week in April, the majority have reached the nesting grounds, though some arrive in May. Some winter as far south as southern Mexico.

BREEDING BIOLOGY

Most ruddy duck hens choose to nest over water on mats of vegetation, which they sometimes weave with overhead canopies. Males tend to stay with the hen a long time—sometimes even after the ducklings hatch. They choose both large and small wetlands as nest sites—the quality of cover seems to determine the choice. Ruddy ducks feed primarily on vegetable foods, though animal matter makes up a significant portion of their diet at certain times and locations.

Ruddy ducks are late nesters, and the peak of nesting in some areas may not occur until early to mid-June. The average clutch is 8.5 eggs, but ruddies are notorious parasitic egg layers, dumping eggs in the nests of both other ruddies and other species. Their eggs are huge—as big as those of wild turkeys—and it is believed that the ruddy lays a larger egg relative to body size than any other duck. Eggs take about 25 days to hatch, and young ruddies fly at six or seven weeks of age. Because they nest so late, and because of the large commitment of nutrient and energy resources to lay such imposing eggs, renesting is probably infrequent.

Whistling Ducks

Tribe Dendrocygnini

There are eight species of whistling ducks worldwide, only two of which, the fulvous whistling duck and the black-bellied whistling duck, are found in North America, and those only in small numbers in the U.S. All whistling ducks belong to the genus *Dendrocygna*, which loosely translates to "tree-swan." Anatomically, whistling ducks share characteristics of swans and geese. They have, for instance, polygonal scales on their lower legs that, unlike ducks' legs, are not arranged in linear rows. Like swans and geese, too, whistling ducks form long pair bonds, the sexes are identical (or nearly so) in plumage, the male helps rear the brood, they have long legs situated near the center of the body, and they are fond of feeding in fields.

Whistling ducks are further different from all other ducks in that the two sexes' whistling vocalizations are nearly identical; they have short, rounded wings and long legs that trail behind the tail when in flight, and most species are able to perch in trees. Whistling ducks are quite gregarious and commonly call to one another in flight. Whistling ducks are both ground nesters and cavity nesters, with the black-bellied whistling duck showing a preference for tree cavity nest sites that are close to water.

FULVOUS WHISTLING DUCK PAIR: ©CLIFF BEITTEL

FULVOUS WHISTLING DUCK

Dendrocygna bicolor
Common Names: Mexican squealer, squealer
Average length—18 inches
Average weight—1.75 pounds

Looking more like a goose than a duck, the fulvous whistling duck has a flattened crown to its head that is distinctive, as well as a short tail. They walk without a waddle, are swift runners, and sometimes perch in trees. They are the most widespread of whistling ducks worldwide, found in North and South America, Africa, and the Indian subcontinent.

Fulvous whistling ducks are handsome, rusty brown birds, with a dark brown back mottled with rust in the forward half. Sexes are nearly identical. Side feathers are ivory edged, yielding an attractive border between sides and back. A white neck patch is visible beneath the chin. The bill, feet, and legs are all dark blue gray. The exceptionally large feet have sharp claws for perching in trees. In flight, the long legs trail behind the duck as they do on ibis. With relatively short, rounded wings, they are slow flying, though maneuver through trees with skill. The tops of the wings are nearly all gray, but the leading edge (lesser covert) is brown.

Very vocal ducks, they call incessantly while flying, emitting a two-note *pee-chee* squeal. They are fond of cultivated rice, and also feed on aquatic vegetation both by swimming and diving.

RANGE AND MIGRATION

In North America, their breeding range includes both coasts of Mexico, with scattered populations in the Mexican highlands and into California, Texas, and Louisiana. They have occasionally been seen (but not breeding) in North Carolina and Florida.

Most are nonmigratory, but those breeding in Texas and Louisiana move south to Tamaulipas, Mexico, by mid-January.

BREEDING BIOLOGY

Fulvous whistling ducks breed at one year of age, and form long pair bonds like geese. Ground nesting is more common in North America than elsewhere in its range, and here they prefer to nest on levees surrounding rice fields or over water among weeds in rice fields. In more natural environments, they choose nest sites in dense vegetation near or over water, where they build mounds that rise several inches above the water's surface. They may also utilize tree cavities.

Clutches average 12 eggs, but dump nesting is frequent. Incubation lasts about 25 days, and both sexes may take turns incubating. In Louisiana, they begin nesting as early as May, but some may nest into August. Both sexes fend for the ducklings, which reach flight stage in about 60 days.

BLACK-BELLIED WHISTLING DUCK PAIR: ©CLIFF BEITTEL

BLACK-BELLIED WHISTLING DUCK

Dendrocygna autumnalis
Common Names: Black-bellied tree duck, black-belly, cornfield duck, pichichi
Average length—19 inches
Average weight—1.8 pounds

With its bright red bill and coral red legs, the black-bellied whistling duck is an unmistakable waterfowl. Comfortable flying through forests, these ducks are seldom far from trees, and when disturbed, frequently choose to perch on branches. Their long necks allow them to exploit vegetation deep beneath the surface of the water, which they do while tipping up like dabbling ducks. They are also fond of feeding in farm fields, and will even perch on cornstalks. Largely nocturnal feeders, their loud *pee-chee-chee* call has yielded their Spanish name, *pichiguila*.

Handsome, cocoa-colored ducks that stand erect, they have a buff-colored face and head with a dark band down the crest and neck, a white ring around their dark eyes, and as the name implies, a black belly. Sexes are identical. In flight, their upper wings show the bright white patches of their coverts that extend nearly to the primaries. Hatchlings are bright yellow with bold black horizontal stripes, but they become gray as they grow older. Black-bellied whistling ducks are seen mostly in pairs or small flocks.

RANGE AND MIGRATION

In North America it ranges from Louisiana and southern Texas south along both coasts of Mexico, but it is far more common in Central and South America.

The black-bellied whistling duck's U.S. range has been expanding in recent years, though the causes are uncertain. Beginning in the 1950s, its range in Texas enlarged from the lower Rio Grande valley northward to Lake Corpus Christi, where the newly impounded lake killed standing trees, which provided suitable nesting cavities. The ducks are also now common breeders along the Texas central gulf coast and the rice prairie areas southwest of Houston. In recent years, they have been spotted as far north as Dallas and even into Arkansas and Oklahoma.

Largely sedentary throughout most of their range, the few that breed in the U.S. probably migrate the short distance to Mexico during the winter.

BREEDING BIOLOGY

Black-bellied whistling ducks mate for life, and breed at one year of age. Although they will nest on the ground, they prefer to nest in tree cavities, like the wood duck. They will also use artificial nest boxes.

Clutch sizes are large, averaging about 13 eggs, but dump nesting is not unusual. Both sexes incubate the eggs, which take about 31 days to hatch. Both parents also take care of the brood, and stay with them well beyond the flight stage, which is reached in about 53 to 63 days. They apparently renest occasionally even if the first attempt was successful.